Contributors

Steve Baldwin   Consultant Psychologist,
Neighbourhood Networks Project,
TACADE/Charity Project.

Ken Barrie   Director, Alcohol Studies Centre,
Paisley College.

Stewart Collins   Senior Lecturer in Social Work,
The Queen's College, Glasgow.

Graham Fanti   Director, Alcohol Advisory Service,
Worcester.

Rosemary Kent   Lecturer, Alcohol Interventions Unit,
University of Kent.

*Tom Leckie**   Adviser, Social Work Services Group,
Edinburgh.

*Gill Ottley**   Adviser, Social Work Services Group,
Edinburgh.

Mary Wilson   Project Leader, Possilpark Addiction Centre,
Glasgow.

*Please note that the contributions of the above do not reflect the policies
of the SWSG.

Introduction

As this book is being written, alcohol-related problems are receiving a great deal of attention in the media. Newspapers, television, and radio regularly include items which warn about the dangers of excessive drink. Riotous scenes during the 1989 European Football Championship have been seen as taking place largely as a result of alcohol-induced loss of inhibition. Attention has been directed towards the so-called 'lager louts' and 'rural riots' whereby small, apparently sleepy towns have been disrupted by drunken rowdiness. Indeed, press reports on the 1988 annual meeting of the Association of Chief Constables were dominated by concern over this matter. But this is not the whole story, and we should be wary of becoming preoccupied with so-called 'drunken hooliganism'. This can shift focus away from those with alcohol problems who do not figure prominently in the media. They can be young women, young parents, and the middle-aged and elderly, who are rarely involved in fights and public-disorder offences. In these instances the damage caused by problem drinking is altogether a more private affair – often silent, closeted, and unpublicised.

Society expresses markedly ambivalent attitudes towards alcohol. If, on the one hand, the mass media condemn excessive use of alcohol, on the other, it actively promotes its use. Alcohol is often associated with status, power, conviviality, attractiveness, and achievement. For instance, it has been estimated that while formal advertising of alcohol takes up approximately thirty *minutes* per week, 'the portrayal of drinking occasions in soap opera or other fictional programmes on TV takes up thirteen *hours* per week and . . . during peak viewing hours alcohol is displayed at the rate of three scenes per hour' (Royal College of Psychiatrists 1986).

Alcohol makes a formidable impact on our lives, for good and ill. We use drink to celebrate significant occasions, to drown our sorrows, and as a reaction to unresolved problems. Alcohol can be

1

relaxing and conducive to congenial discussion. Thus alcohol is associated with pleasure. But it can also cause a good deal of personal and social harm when taken to excess. We condemn excessively wild, uninhibited, unruly, and thoughtless behaviour when 'under the influence'. Loud voices raised in argument, physical violence, collapse, and vomiting after drinking are usually censured by those who remain sober. We are, therefore, both critical of the negative effects of alcohol and content to emblazon its positive effects.

Alcohol problems seem to be an accepted part of society's problems. There is an attitude of 'Most of us drink, drink isn't much of a problem really . . . there are far more serious things'. Heroin, AIDS, and child abuse are all topics seen to be more noteworthy: to be more often in the public eye and to require an immediate response from government. No-one could deny the seriousness of these matters and the urgent need for action. However, in comparison, alcohol problems tend to produce a low-key response of 'Oh they're only drunk . . . they've just had a few too many', accompanied by a shrug of the shoulders. The idea of drink as a problem for large numbers of people in significant proportions is played down. Hence there is a strong tendency to deny the amount of harm caused by drink. In recent years there has been much research evidence to suggest that the overall drinking level of a nation plays a very large part in determining the overall levels of harm; when consumption per head rises, so do all the well-known indicators of harm. For instance, when UK consumption declined between 1979 and 1982, there was also an overall reduction in the adverse effects of alcohol, such as convictions for drunkenness, drunk driving, and first admissions to hospital for alcohol dependence.

Despite mounting evidence to the contrary there is still a readiness to present alcohol-related problems linked only to 'alcoholism' and 'the alcoholic' without considering that, in fact, these labels represent the *last* stage of a long continuum of problems linked to alcohol-related harm. Abundant evidence is available of the extent to which alcohol-related harm is associated with accidents, work problems, crime, physical and mental ill health, and relationship problems. It has been suggested that alcohol-related harm may be associated with 62 per cent of serious head injuries in males, 45 per cent of fatal road traffic accidents involving pedestrians, 33 per cent of all domestic accidents, and 30 per cent of drownings (Saunders 1984). It has also been suggested that between 8 million and 14 million working days are lost in Great Britain each year on account of alcohol misuse and that the financial cost in England

and Wales of such absences has been estimated as being close to £1.5m each year (McDonnell and Maynard 1985).

In attempting to estimate the incidence of alcohol-related crime there are difficulties in defining what is meant by an alcohol-related offence and variations in local policy. However, in one recent investigation, 64 per cent of those arrested had been drinking in the four hours previous to their arrest, while between 10 p.m. and 2 p.m., 93 per cent of all the arrested persons were intoxicated (Jeffs and Saunders 1983). Also, recent British studies have indicated that between 30 per cent and 50 per cent of burglaries were committed while the offender was under the influence of alcohol while overall, between 1970 and 1982, rates of conviction for drunkenness rose by almost 25 per cent (Royal College of Psychiatrists 1986; Plant *et al.* 1985).

To this catalogue of catastrophe can be added the contribution of alcohol-related harm to mental health problems. For instance, it has been estimated that problem drinkers are 40–50 times more likely to commit suicide, while 66 per cent of parasuicides are likely to have alcohol problems (Alcohol Concern 1987; Saunders 1984). Detailed evidence could be provided also for a massive correlation between alcohol-related problems and physical illnesses – such as the greater likelihood of the problem drinker experiencing liver damage, stomach problems, heart troubles, high blood pressure, and last, but not least, the foetal alcohol syndrome. Even now this growing compendium of harm would not be complete without considering the high incidence of drinking in stressful marital relationships, wife battering, and child abuse. All these matters will be considered further in Chapters 4 and 5.

What is also particularly startling is the social cost of drinking. In Great Britain, while our consumption of alcohol doubled between the 1950s and the late 1970s, the real cost of drink was reduced by more than half during the same period. For example, it took twenty-three minutes to earn the cost of a pint of beer thirty years ago; now it requires only eleven minutes (Royal College of Psychiatrists 1986; Alcohol Concern 1988). What is more, the cost of drink is likely to fall even further; in 1992 the UK will be forced to cut its duty on drink in line with the rest of the European Economic Community.

In 1985 we spent nearly £16,000 bn on alcohol; the equivalent of £369 for every adult in Britain. This was more than the money we spend on clothes, more than the Government spends on hospitals or schools; and only just less than the national defence budget (Alcohol Concern 1988). Thus alcohol draws in an extraordinary amount of income from the consumer. It is big business; it is one of our major industries in that:

The Brewers Society estimates that the industry provides over £2,200 million in farmers' incomes; uses about half the total number of bottles produced in the country; employs three quarters of a million people in production, distribution and retailing; contributes almost £500 million to the balance of trade and the Government receives over 5% of its total income from excise duty and value added tax on drinks.

(Thurman 1981: 9–14).

Thus it is against this kind of economic background that State policies are drawn up. There is clearly a heavy investment in the production and generation of wealth by the alcohol industry and this is a major source of employment and tax revenue in Great Britain. Dorn has expressed this most succinctly:

Whatever political muscle may be put behind arguments about what the State 'ought' to do to restrict production and total consumption, the State's policies on alcohol production are *actually* conditioned by its broader concerns with private profitability and electoral and fiscal considerations.

(Dorn 1983: 71)

It should therefore be made clear that alcohol-related problems exist within an economic, political, and social context. Equally, if problem drinking takes place within economic and social parameters, then harm is also evident within those parameters. It has been conservatively estimated that damage from alcohol-related problems stood at £1,614 m at 1983 prices (McDonnell and Maynard 1985). At 1987 prices that would be around £2 bn pounds per year, while it has been suggested that taking into account home accidents, damage by fire, and the demands placed on social workers and probation officers, the figures could well add up to £10 bn (Alcohol Concern 1988).

What is the impact of alcohol-related problems upon social workers? Available evidence is limited, but a number of studies have produced some disturbing findings, which are also considered in Chapter 2. There is clearly a substantial proportion of social work clients who *are* experiencing alcohol-related problems. Yet at the same time a number of studies also indicate that social workers lack knowledge and confidence in this area, often resort to stereotyping, wonder if intervention is justified or may be a waste of time, and prefer to be excessively reliant upon general practitioners or psychiatrists (Robinson 1976; Bardell *et al.* 1981; Murray 1985; Cartwright *et al.* 1975; Isaacs and Moon 1985). Nor do workers seem to feel that social work courses adequately prepare them; a recent study of Hampshire social workers indicated that almost 75 per cent of the workers believed they had received no specific education or training for 'treatment and care' of the problem drinker (Isaacs and Moon 1985). After qualification, evidence that is available indicates there is a lack of support from within the agency context, and the supervision which is provided is inadequate (Shaw *et al.* 1978). This, in turn, leads to further insecurity for the worker.

Therefore, one of the specific purposes of this book is to help social workers develop confidence in their existing knowledge and skills when working with clients who have alcohol-related problems in individual, marital, family, and group contexts. However, there have been so many rapid developments in the field of counselling problem drinkers in recent years that a second purpose of the book is to help the reader become more aware of new knowledge and skills which can inform and help their day-to-day practice.

While this book focuses upon alcohol problems, it should be noted that there is a growing movement which encourages consideration of a number of similarities between addictive behaviours generally. The reasons for addictive behaviour, the problems that are likely to occur, the difficulties that are experienced in stopping, all have much in common. As practitioners, we can develop our knowledge and skills by studying these 'commonalities' and benefiting from a cross-fertilisation of ideas shared by excessive appetites for food, sex, drug use, and drinking (Orford 1985). While these matters will be considered throughout the book, the prime focus will remain sharply and clearly upon problem drinking.

First of all, we begin with an examination of the background against which many social workers operate. In Chapter 1 Stewart Collins, Gill Ottley, and Mary Wilson provide a brief historical perspective on the use of alcohol but, in particular, they examine the development in the post-war years of Alcohol Treatment Units and community services for problem drinkers in the voluntary sector. The contribution of Alcoholics Anonymous is examined, as well as the more recent growth of Councils on Alcohol. Finally, the significance of organisational and interagency co-operative ventures is emphasised.

The part played by statutory social work in assisting problem drinkers is considered by Tom Leckie in Chapter 2. Interventions by the individual social worker are firmly located within an agency context. Leckie highlights the need for informed supervision of social workers and calls for an adequate response to alcohol-related problems from all parts of the agency hierarchy. The chapter goes on to examine the established knowledge and skills which social workers already possess that can be used in order to work effectively with problem drinkers and thus help social workers overcome some of their fears about intervening in such situations. This includes the use of systems approaches, Rogerian counselling, crisis intervention, and task-centred work. Leckie moves on to consider the difficult choices which face a social worker in deciding whether to work alone with a client or in conjunction with another agency, or simply to hand over entirely to another agency. He concludes by examining some of the recent developments in interagency collaboration.

There have been a number of recent innovations in helping individual problem drinkers and in Chapter 3, Steve Baldwin draws upon the work of social-learning theorists. He argues for more specific assessments and goal setting around alcohol-related problems. He asks readers to consider a variety of helping styles that are available in the field of counselling problem drinkers and then examines the significance of relapse, the place of controlled drinking; and the role of minimal interventions and alcohol education courses.

Gender issues have received particular attention in social work literature in recent years. In Chapter 4 Rosemary Kent looks at these issues in relation to problem drinking. Her chapter demands that social workers examine their attitudes to female problem drinkers in the context of women's disadvantaged position in society as a whole. She argues that it is important to have a social and political understanding of women's vulnerability when involved in drinking situations. Rosemary Kent goes on to emphasise the feelings of ambivalence and conflict which may be experienced by both female clients and social workers when considering the disclosure of drinking problems and the behavioural changes that are then sought. The chapter concludes with an examination of various aspects of alcohol-related problems in women and includes some suggestions for appropriate intervention by social workers.

Much social work involves contact with families. In Chapter 5 Graham Fanti looks closely at families with members who are experiencing alcohol problems. He considers the physical, psychological, and social difficulties encountered by such families and the roles and relationships within the families. Fanti suggests that families move through various stages of crisis and coping. He provides a striking case example. Difficulties which the worker might encounter are considered, as well as some strategies for helping in the pre-action, action, and follow-up stages.

Traditionally a great deal of the help available to problem

drinkers has been through the medium of groups. In the final chapter, Ken Barrie considers these perspectives; he suggests some of the positive contributions which group work can offer, such as mutual support and learning. Barrie then examines selection criteria and some stages of change that may be expected to occur in groups for those with alcohol problems. He goes on to provide an outline for the content of a short group programme, which should be of considerable practical assistance to social workers.

During the process of putting the book together, a persistent theme which runs through the writing of all the contributors has become evident – the importance of the provision of community services for problem drinkers. This is not to deny the crucial contribution of hospital treatment and residential provision on some occasions, but so many of the difficulties which problem drinkers encounter have to be faced by social workers and probation officers in the community – in area team settings. It is the problems of these drinkers and their social workers that are our particular concern.

Also, we would not want to underestimate the many demands faced by social workers in their day-to-day tasks. Much local authority social work is carried out under almost siege-like conditions – caseloads are increasing and financial resources are being cut back. Social workers are required to respond to different priorities as changes in political analyses of social problems occur and as fashions in various types of intervention rise and fall. Dictates of the agency, the profession, legislation, and the media all impose powerful, and sometimes conflicting, forces upon individual social workers. Alcohol abuse is a constant element in a world which contains many and varied social problems. It poses thorny and difficult questions which require some answers from social work – and more satisfactory answers than have been provided up to now.

Stewart Collins,
Milton by Dumbarton,
Dumbarton, Scotland.

References

Alcohol Concern (1987) *Teaching about Alcohol Problems*, Cambridge: Woodhead-Faulkner.

Alcohol Concern (1988) *The Drinking Revolution*, Cambridge: Woodhead-Faulkner.

Bardell, L., Lamont, F., Leckie, T., and Osborne, A. (1981) *Alcohol-related Problems in Current Social Work Cases*, Edinburgh: Lothian Regional Council Social Work Department.

Introduction

Cartwright, A., Shaw, S., and Spratley, T. (1975) *Designing a Comprehensive Community Response to Problems of Alcohol Abuse*, London: The Maudsley Hospital.

Dorn, N. (1983) *Alcohol, Youth and the State*, London: Croom Helm.

Isaacs, J. and Moon, G. (1985) *Alcohol Problems – the Social Work Response*, Portsmouth: Social Services Research and Intelligence Unit.

Jeffs, B. and Saunders, W. (1983) 'Minimising alcohol related offences by enforcement of existing licensing legislation', *British Journal of Addiction* 78 (1):67–77.

McDonnell, R. and Maynard, A. (1985) 'The costs of alcohol misuse', *British Journal of Addiction* 80:27–36.

Murray, N. (1985) 'Time, social workers, please', *Community Care*, 15 August, pp. 12–14.

Plant, M., Peck, D., and Samuel, E. (1985) *Alcohol, Drugs and School Leavers*, London: Tavistock.

Robinson, D. (1976) *From Drinking To Alcoholism*, Chichester: John Wiley.

Royal College of Psychiatrists (1986) *Alcohol: Our Favourite Drug*, London: Tavistock.

Saunders, W. (1984) 'Alcohol use in Britain: how much is too much?', *Health Education Journal* 43 (2 and 3):66–70.

Shaw, S., Cartwright, A., Spratley, T., and Harwin, J. (1978) *Responding to Drinking Problems*, London: Croom Helm.

Thurman, C. (1981) 'The structure and role of the alcoholic drinks industry', London: Brewers Society, unpublished mimeo.

Chapter one

Historical perspectives and the development of community services

Stewart Collins, Gill Ottley, and Mary Wilson

We do not intend to provide a detailed, historical perspective on the subject of alcohol consumption, control, and abuse – rather to outline briefly some of the trends that can be seen in the drinking of alcohol in Great Britain during the past 300 years. In particular, we shall examine the development of community services for problem drinkers in the recent, post-war years. For more detailed accounts, which between them encompass the necessary moral, political, and economic perspectives, the reader is referred to the works of several authors (Harrison 1971; Hawkins and Pass 1979; Mathias 1979; Williams and Brake 1980; Dorn 1983; Heather and Robertson 1985).

At the outset it must be said that drinking of alcoholic beverages has a very long history, dating back to the earliest human civilisations. Sumerian physicians and Egyptian doctors prescribed beer and wine as a cure for illnesses around the year 2000 BC. Also alcohol has always played a prominent part in the celebration of significant events of various kinds such as births, deaths, marriages, anniversaries, and religious ceremonies. In fact, the part played by wine was very important in the religions of the Greeks and Romans and still plays a significant symbolic role in the Christian Eucharist.

Our main concern is to focus upon the use of alcohol in Great Britain as:

> Alcohol is the chosen intoxicant of European peoples. . . . It has been part of our lives from the very beginning of our civilisation and it is woven inextricably into our culture. . . . We drink to celebrate more personal triumphs and to drown our sorrows too. . . . We drink to give ourselves an appetite, to help us relax, to mark the end of the working day, to prove that we are grown up, assert our virility, to help us get to sleep. The list is almost endless.
>
> (Royal College of Psychiatrists 1986:18)

As well as generating positive feelings, the use of alcohol has produced strikingly negative, critical feelings and in Great Britain attitudes towards alcohol have often been fluid and changeable at various stages in history. There have been swings between the extremes of regarding it as a source of much harmless pleasure and, alternatively, of seeing it as a remarkable threat to public decency and order (Heather and Robertson 1985). Equally, in the last 300 years there have been marked changes in the actual consumption of alcohol, with dramatic differences in the consumption of individual beverages such as beer, spirits, and wine. It is, of course, well known that in the seventeenth and eighteenth centuries beer consumption per capita was much higher than it was in the nineteenth century and early twentieth century and, indeed, than it is at the present time. A beer duty had been first imposed in 1643 and the earliest national records of consumption date from 1684. Beer consumption reached an all-time maximum of 832 pints per person per year – i.e. 2.2 pints per person per day – in 1689 (Spring and Buss 1977). In part, such high levels of consumption were associated with the fact that in most parts of the country, beer was less likely to be contaminated with sewerage than the water supply. Also the ale house was the centre of working life. It was used as a labour exchange, it was a site for the court – and the local transport interchange. Drunkenness was a more 'normal' and 'acceptable' state. Hence the often quoted remark of Dr Johnson, recalling his early years when: 'All the decent people of Lichfield got drunk every night, so were not the worse thought of' (Heather and Robertson 1985:22).

It should not be implied that drunkenness was entirely without censure and punishment before the nineteenth century, even though it was not seen as a major problem. Magistrates were empowered to fine offenders, have them whipped, placed in the stocks, and even imprisoned. However, in rural areas at least, the social control imposed by local community ties and norms generally acted as sufficient deterrent.

In urban areas, during the seventeenth century, some have argued that controls focused upon public houses were aimed more at suppressing the opportunities for working-class people to meet for political and recreational activities rather than arising from a concern about the control of alcohol consumption (Dorn 1983). It was only in the 1720s that drinking habits themselves started to become a cause for concern, with the easy availability of cheap gin, costing one penny a pint, in London and other urban centres. Subsequently, a 1751 Act greatly increased duty and placed restraints on the sale of spirits, while further legislation – the 1752

Disorderly Houses Act – controlled the excessive number of public houses. At the same time these pieces of legislation were somewhat isolated islands in a sea of non-intervention. Throughout the seventeenth and most of the eighteenth century the predominant philosophical perspectives encouraged a view of human beings as rational, reasoning entities who acted in accordance with principles of self-interest. In other words, choice was exercised: 'drunkenness was a choice, albeit a sinful one, which some individuals made' (Levine 1978:146). It was believed people chose to be drunk and were assumed to be fully aware of any consequences which might result; more detailed, complex explanations of drunkenness were not thought necessary, only correction by punishment or occasional legislation.

Consumption levels did not rise significantly in the nineteenth century, as the industrial revolution progressed and the population became more centred upon the developing manufacturing towns. Nevertheless, drinking of alcohol began to be viewed as much more problematic. It has been suggested that intoxication at work in an industrialised society was now far more likely to restrict profit levels, to endanger both the overall production process, and inhibit or prevent the work of others (Dorn 1983). In addition, the breakdown of a society previously based largely upon agriculture brought with it a new social order which presented both challenge and threat to the traditions of existing institutions.

Alcohol was seen as part of that threat. Others have suggested that at the time of the industrial revolution drinking alcohol became associated with 'disreputable' working-class lifestyles, accompanied by a lack of self-control and lack of thrift (Gusfield 1963). This was taken further during the late 1700s and early 1800s in the pioneering writings of Benjamin Rush in the United States and Thomas Trotter in Scotland. They began to provide scientific explanations for understanding excessive drinking promulgating, for the first time, the idea of alcohol as a disease, an addictive substance over which the individual had no control and could not exercise choice or free will. These ideas were used by the Temperance Movement, which began to emerge from the 1830s onwards as a particularly powerful and significant force. Initially the focus was upon forgiveness, compassion, mutual aid, education, and treatment. Therefore Protestant non-conformist movements played a large part in the drive against the 'evils of drink'. In the late 1800s and early 1900s the Temperance Movement was at its height, by now placing an increased emphasis on the need for legislative controls. By 1900 it had 3 million members – almost one in four of the relevant age group. As a consequence, by the time of the First

World War alcohol was seen to pose a very serious threat to established order. The outbreak of the war exaggerated this concern. A new peak was reached in the range of State interventions in the alcohol field to improve social discipline and industrial productivity. Numerous controls were imposed to restrict opening hours, to restrain the numbers of licensed premises, and, on one of those rare occasions, actually to *reduce* the production of alcohol and the gravity of beer. In fact, between 1914 and 1918, beer consumption fell by no less than 63 per cent and spirits consumption by 52 per cent (Royal College of Psychiatrists 1986).

Consumption rose again at the end of the First World War only to fall once more during the economic problems and struggles of the 1930s, remaining at a relatively low level until the 1950s (Williams and Brake 1980). During this period the ill effects of alcohol were much less in evidence, the Temperance Movement lost much of its power, and the number of total abstainers began to decline. Legislative constraints were also less evident. The recent Royal College of Psychiatrists Report (1986) commented that:

> Thirty years ago in this country alcohol dependence . . . was seen as something that did not have much to do with our own century, and a condition from which the British were . . . deemed to be immune. The indifference of the general public was matched by lack of interest among the professions: medical schools taught only about the physical complications of advanced alcohol abuse; the NHS made no special provisions for treatment; and there was no special nursing or social work interest. Government Departments saw no need for action. The nation's drinking problems were passively ignored or purposely denied.
>
> (Royal College of Psychiatrists 1986: 24)

The rise of the 'disease' model: some criticisms

This state of affairs in Great Britain in the 1950s stood in contrast to the situation in the United States, where the end of prohibition and the birth of Alcoholics Anonymous had encouraged a transition towards the view of alcoholism as a disease. Developments based upon the Yale Centre for Alcohol Studies accelerated this process. Academics, representatives from Alcoholics Anonymous, the liquor industry, and the Temperance Movement came together with the National Council of Alcohol to form what was collectively known as 'The Alcoholism Movement'. Pressures were imposed to ensure that alcoholism was recognised as a disease and, although having approved the inclusion of alcoholism in its official nomenclature of disease in the 1930s, the American Medical Association really developed a more vigorous and aggressive approach to this matter in the 1950s. The Association stated they recognised the 'syndrome of alcoholism as an illness which justifiably should have the attention of physicians' (quoted in Heather and Robertson 1985:47). The World Health Organization had also been pressing for additional attention to be given to alcohol problems since the 1950s.

As a result of these various influences, changes began to occur in Great Britain. The first Alcohol Treatment Unit had been established by Max Glatt at Workingham Park Hospital in southern England in the early 1950s; in the early 60s the first Scottish Unit was set up in Edinburgh, and a new unit opened in Wales around that time. Finally, in 1962 a Ministry of Health memorandum recommended the setting up of hospital-based units for the treatment of alcoholism.

The 1962 Ministry of Health memorandum emphasised in-patient care, although the value of out-patient help and links with Alcoholics Anonymous was noted. The prevailing model encouraged perceptions of alcoholism primarily as a disease, an illness, that required institutional treatment of an intensive and long-term nature. The 'disease' approach undoubtedly carried some positive connotations. It ensured a better helping service for those with drink problems; it ensured the provision of assistance beyond the nihilism of a prison sentence; it may have produced a more sympathetic attitude amongst family members, friends, and employers (Room 1984). In particular, it initiated a more benign, tolerant, and understanding attitude from a medical standpoint and led to the development of quite extensive research endeavours.

It should be made clear that there are several perspectives on the definition of alcoholism as a disease. E.M. Jellinek in his classic study of disease theory commented on no less than 115 distinct ways in which alcoholism had been so described (Jellinek 1960). We would suggest, however, that there are several common features of the disease model which seem worthy of emphasis. First, the alcoholic was seen to crave for drink, lose control, and present behaviour which was beyond the realm of choice. In other words, some individuals were thought to be predisposed to drink problems; it was not drink that was a problem – it was the personality of the drinker. Second, alcoholism was seen as a discrete entity in that those suffering from it were seen as intrinsically different from those not suffering in that way. Third, the loss of control over alcohol and continued craving for it was seen as irreversible; alcoholism could not be cured, only arrested, on account of biological or psychological abnormalities which made 'normal' drinking impossible. Therefore the alcoholic should be compelled towards commitment to total and life-long abstinence. In addition, if not 'treated', the alcoholic would deteriorate further and treatment became absolutely essential.

These tenets have been strongly challenged in recent years. Much research has shown that it is very difficult to distinguish between a fixed population of 'alcoholics' and 'non-alcoholics'. It is now accepted that problem drinking exists on a continuum, with normal or non-problem drinking at one end and severe dependence at the other. Hence: 'there is no single constellation of alcohol related problems which can be described as alcoholism. Rather there is a range of problems – medical, legal, occupational, social, marital or interpersonal which can be experienced by those who drink excessively' (Heather and Robertson 1986:117).

Many studies have shown that 'normal drinking' can be resumed after treatment, although clearly a significant number of serious problem drinkers would be well advised to abstain totally (Heather and Robertson 1981). Ideas about loss of control and craving are also now seen as unhelpful: there is no evidence that these are irreversible trends. This has been demonstrated in rigorous, empirical studies of diagnosed 'chronic alcoholics' returning to moderate drinking behaviour over both short- and long-term follow-up periods (Armor *et al.* 1978; Pollich *et al.* 1980; Sobell and Sobell 1978). Studies in controlled conditions, when alcohol was freely available to alcoholics, have also revealed that the subjects did not demonstrate an uncontrollable urge to drink (Mello and Mendelson 1965; Mello *et al.* 1968). Furthermore, on the evidence of random 'household surveys' it becomes impossible to distinguish between so-called out-of-control alcoholic drinking and so-called non-alcoholic drinking in the community (Cahalan 1970). Neither is there evidence of an inevitable, progressive deterioration when drinking is continued and, whilst treatment may be sometimes helpful, the impact of life events such as marriage, the birth of children, and new employment opportunities are seen as particularly significant (Roizen *et al.* 1978; Armor *et al.* 1978; Saunders and Kershaw 1979; Tuchfeld 1976; Vaillant 1983).

There were further disadvantages to the disease approach. The emphasis given to providing better treatment facilities in institutional settings has been often at the expense of working upon the prevention of drinking problems in the community. Furthermore, an excessive weighting was given to the perception of alcohol problems as a province for medical specialists rather than an arena for psychological and social work intervention and voluntary effort. As persons labelled alcoholic often became institutionalised and 'ill', so they perceived themselves, and were perceived by others, as 'sick' and therefore not responsible. In other words, passive co-operation became the order of the day and the medical expert took over responsibility for care and treatment.

One final, significant, aspect of the process inherent in the disease approach is that attention becomes focused upon the more serious problem drinker, the dependent problem drinker. The most dramatic features of problem drinking are emphasised, the most serious physical and social consequences. Unfortunately, this subsequently leads to a neglect of the vast majority of the drinking population who are *not* severely dependent, who are moderate or heavy drinkers, who are younger (often in their late teens or twenties) and who do not wish to abstain. The setting of abstinence goals for such groups generally reveals a high failure rate and research evidence clearly shows that younger problem drinkers are very likely to find it particularly difficult to maintain abstinence (Armor *et al.* 1978). Indeed, the population in Alcohol Treatment Units is usually aged over 40 and attenders at Alcoholics Anonymous also tend to be in this age range. The disease approach rules out the possibility of controlled drinking and makes it difficult to draw in for help problem drinkers who may be guilty of numerous instances of nuisance behaviour *before* serious personal and social damage has occurred. It now seems evident that for some people who are not dependent problem drinkers, medical help may be irrelevant. Non-judgemental counselling and clear advice and guidance may be what is required in order to encourage a problem drinker to weigh up the advantages and disadvantages of their life-style, resolve the resultant conflict, and lead on to a reduction in consumption.

In fact, the provision of longer term, short-term, and self-help procedures can be appropriately located in community settings. A number of front-line workers or primary-care workers, such as social workers, probation officers, health visitors, volunteers, and nurses are well placed to offer this sort of help. It will later become evident that they are already significantly skilled in the field of alcohol problems and have the ability to intervene effectively.

To sum up, then, at this stage we are arguing that the harm caused by excessive drinking exists on a continuum; different degrees of harm require different kinds of responses. The disease approach concentrates attention on the most serious and chronic dependent drinkers, but both the regular heavy user and those who become intoxicated from time to time can also benefit from helping interventions. We would now like to consider the use of units and drinking 'levels'.

Units and drinking levels

Standard measures of most popular drinks served in public houses contain roughly the same amount of alcohol. A half pint of ordinary bitter, lager, or cider; a glass of wine, sherry, or port, or a single measure of spirits all contain about 8–10 grams of alcohol. Therefore each of these items can be regarded as one standard unit. $\frac{1}{2}$ pint of beer = 1 glass of wine = 1 single measure of spirits = one unit of alcohol.

Clearly, however, the 'strengths' of some drinks will vary and we should consider the following:

Drinks	*Units*
1 pint of ordinary beer or lager	= 2
1 pint of Guinness, some 'real' ales, or strong lager	= 3
1 pint of strong cider (e.g. Blackthorn or Strongbow)	= 4
1 can of ordinary beer or lager	= $1\frac{1}{2}$
1 can 'Special lager'	= 3
1 glass of sparkling wine or strong wine	= 2
1 bottle of table wine	= 7
1 litre bottle of table wine	= 10
1 bottle of sherry or port	= 14
1 bottle of spirits (whisky, gin, vodka)	= 30

Table 1.1   Drinking levels

	Men (units per week)	% of adult population	Women (units per week)	% of adult population
Light drinking, safe for health	1–21	54	1–14	52
Moderate drinking	22–25	6	15–21	1
Regular, fairly heavy drinking, harm to health is likely	36–50	6	22–35	1
Regular, very heavy drinking, definitely damaging to health	51+	6	36+	1

Source: Office of Population Censuses and Survey, Davis 1989.

While the main medical authorities and health promotion bodies appear to be agreed on the recommended limits for 'sensible drinking i.e. no more than 21 units per week for men and no more than 14 units per week for women, there is some disagreement about how regular, heavy drinking should be defined. Table 1.1 is drawn from information provided by the Office of Population Censuses and Surveys (Davis 1989:111). Please note that Table 1.1 excludes non-drinkers and occasional drinkers.

An alternative to the disease model

We would advocate consideration of Thorley's model as an alternative explanatory system.

Thorley's model of problem drug use

Thorley (1985) suggests there is a wide range of problems – social, legal, and medical that relate to intoxication, regular excessive use, and dependence on alcohol. Because the definition of regular excessive use is also problematic, we prefer the term regular heavy use. Thorley's model describes a pattern of drug taking that falls into three elements of behaviour as represented by the circles in Figure 1.1. It would be wrong to assume that the three areas or patterns of problem drug use exist separately and Figure 1.1 shows there may well be overlap between the three drinking patterns. The person who is intoxicated may also regularly drink quantities of alcohol but may not be dependent. The person who drinks regular amounts may be dependent but may not be intoxicated, while the dependent person may regularly drink quantities of alcohol and may also show signs of intoxication. It is probably helpful to look at each of the identified areas in turn.

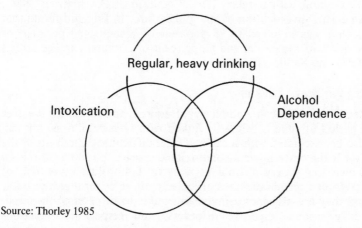

Source: Thorley 1985

Figure 1.1   Thorley's model of problem drug use

17

Intoxication

Intoxication may not be a behaviour which many of us regard as problematic, if it occurs safely within the confines of our own home. Many of us who enjoy social drinking (and this will be the majority of us) will at some time have experienced some of the problems associated with overindulgence and intoxication – such as a hangover. Normally such unpleasant experiences are short-lived and do not have a lasting effect. Indeed, most of us drink alcohol precisely because it intoxicates and moderate doses usually have a pleasant effect. However, consumption of even a moderate dose at the wrong time or in the wrong place can be problematic, for instance, when operating machinery or driving a car. For instance, some people will be over the legal limit for driving (80 mg/100 ml or 80 milligrammes of alcohol in 100 milliletres of blood) after consuming 2.5 pints (5 units) of alcohol and their ability to drive will already be impaired before this limit is reached. The limit was set at this level because this is the point at which driving skills deteriorate rapidly. However, consumption of *any* alcohol will diminish driving skills to some extent and it may be that the legal limit will be far lower in years to come.

On a national level the statistics indicate intoxication is an extremely serious problem. In Scotland research by the Scottish Health Education Co-ordinating Committee (SHECC) has indicated that it 'is strongly associated with parasuicide, fire fatalities, homicide, hospital admission with head injuries and fatal road traffic accidents' (SHECC 1985:xv). Other research associates intoxication with burglary (Royal College of Psychiatrists 1986). An earlier investigation by one police force in England found that alcohol was involved in 78 per cent of assaults, 80 per cent of breaches of the peace, and 88 per cent of criminal damage arrests (Jeffs and Saunders 1983).

Regular heavy drinking

Regular use of alcohol and heavy, frequent, and continued use over a period of time is primarily linked with physical illness, but can also be associated with social and legal difficulties. Cirrhosis of the liver is the best-known alcohol-related disease, but it has also been shown that heavy alcohol users have a 40-fold greater risk of developing certain cancers particularly of the upper digestive tract, and they are also increasingly susceptible to diseases of the circulatory system, digestive disorders, and respiratory infections (Taylor 1981).

British research has indicated that one in five male admissions to general medical wards are related to the patients' use of alcohol (Quinn and Johnstone 1976) and it is also thought that regular, heavy drinking by pregnant women and their associated lifestyle may be detrimental to their unborn children (Plant 1986).

A number of factors will influence the effect that a given amount of alcohol has on an individual, such as how much is taken, how quickly, the size of the person, and whether the drink is taken with food or not. The Royal College of Psychiatrists Report (1986) suggests drinking in excess of 36 or more units a week for men or 22 units a week or more for women is likely to cause some harm, but the whole topic of what constitutes a safe level of consumption is one of continuing debate (Saunders 1984).

It is generally recognised that certain occupations which involve alcohol being freely available have a very high rate of alcohol-related problems, for example, people employed in the production and sale of alcohol, people in the catering and hotel trade, fishermen, members of the merchant navy and armed forces (Plant 1979). At the same time it is worth noting that changes in an individual's consumption can be dramatically influenced by alterations in lifestyle and movement from one job to another can be associated with major changes in consumption (Saunders and Allsop 1985).

Dependence

Dependence or difficulty in refraining from drinking is traditionally the category which includes those persons previously regarded as alcoholics. Both physical and psychological dependence are problematic and the conditions are not mutually exclusive. Physical dependence can cause serious health problems and those who are physically dependent who attempt to reduce or cease use of alcohol may experience withdrawal symptoms. Psychological dependence can also be problematic as drinkers who feel dependent may go to great lengths to obtain more alcohol. Problems associated with dependence may include:

Medical problems	*Social problems*	*Legal problems*
Anxiety	Family problems	Fraud
Phobias	Financial problems	Theft
Depression	Psychological problems	
Hallucinations	Homelessness	
Withdrawal symptoms		
Delirium tremens		
Epilepsy		
Personality change		

19

However, it is relevant to note that the term dependence by itself is generally no longer considered useful without taking into account an understanding of the much more wide-ranging nature of alcohol misuse.

The early development of services to problem drinkers

So far in this chapter we have briefly considered historical perspectives on alcohol-related problems. We have looked at the development of the so-called disease model and the movement away from this model to a more flexible approach, culminating in the work of Anthony Thorley. In looking at the implications of this model for the provision of services for problem drinkers, we will first examine the general development of helping facilities in Great Britain from the end of the Second World War.

The development of specialised alcohol services to combat the 'disease' of alcoholism closely followed the situation in America. Intensive and long-term support, often within an institutional setting was the order of the day. This pattern reflected a societal response to the 'dependence' end of the continuum of problem drinking, to the exclusion of all else. As long as alcoholism was regarded as a progressive, possibly genetically determined disease, services and policies organised to prevent the problem – even at a secondary level – were marked by their absence.

Alcohol Treatment Units (ATUs)

Alcohol Treatment Units, set up in the early 1950s, still represent the major treatment response within the National Health Service. There are over 14,000 admissions annually in England and Wales. There is a heavy emphasis on group work (often involving Alcoholics Anonymous) and, of course, a detoxification facility. Sometimes such facilities encompass educational, training, and research functions, but these were never widely developed. There are now over 30 units in England and Wales and 15 in Scotland. But with growing evidence that expensive in-patient care is no more effective than community-based responses, there are plans in some areas to close them as separate units within hospitals.

In 1948 the drug Antabuse was introduced. This controversial deterrent drug, if combined with alcohol, produces vomiting, sweating, and a general feeling of being unwell. The availability of the drug has encouraged some general practitioners to offer community-based support, even where detoxification is required. But there is legitimate concern that its use undermines the development of self-efficacy in the patient in the long term.

Hostel provision

The institutional provision of ATUs is augmented by a wide range of residential hostel projects accounting for about one-third of alcohol agencies within the voluntary sector. The wider hostel and homeless scene, which owes much to church organisations for its development, also offers support for the problem drinker. It should be noted, however, that problem drinking is more often a consequence rather than a cause of homelessness. The funding for the majority of these projects comes from either voluntary donations with local or central government supplementation, or a sharing of costs between local and central government. In many of these establishments alcohol recovery, rehabilitation, and resocialisation programmes have been initiated, while in others, self-help approaches are the norm.

Alcoholics Anonymous

Alcoholics Anonymous is without doubt the most widely known source of help for problem drinkers. It encompasses a worldwide network of self-help groups which permeates into even the most remote rural areas. The movement has its origins in the USA, with a founding group established in 1935. By 1944 there were 300 groups in the USA and by 1957 over 7,000 throughout the world. Today, a worldwide membership of over 1 million is claimed, with 1,350 AA groups in England and Wales and 25 contact points.

The programme is grounded on the disease model of alcoholism and, as such, focuses on the drinker's weaknesses/pathology *vis-à-vis* alcohol, rather than on the substance itself or the wider environment. The alcoholic is seen as powerless over the progressive course of the illness, as long as he or she continues to ingest alcohol. With each relapse, the consequences are more severe. In Great Britain in the early 1950s, the incidence of problem drinking was at an all-time low, so that a model of the problem as individual pathology was quite fitting. Regular, heavy drinking and intoxication were a rarity and were highly stigmatised, particularly in the case of female drinkers. The principal source of help rested with psychiatric hospitals. Alcoholics Anonymous's guarantee of anonymity, for those professing to be alcoholic, was therefore very apposite and comforting. However, the principle of anonymity is also understood within the fellowship to serve as a means of protecting members from the temptation of using their recovery for personal acclaim through the media or other means.

As a community service for problem drinkers, Alcoholics Anonymous maintains a politically neutral and independent stance by refusing to form any alliances with, or accept any financial and material resources from, any other agency, organisations, or individual from outside its ranks. It does not produce promotional literature as such, nor does it keep records to monitor and evaluate its service. It stresses that problems other than those directly involving alcohol are not within its remit.

Anyone may attend an 'open' Alcoholics Anonymous meeting. It will last for about an hour, and be attended by around 15 to 40 members. The proceedings will be presided over by a 'top-table', including a chairperson and a speaker. The speaker describes his or her own personal problem drinking and recovery history, after which the meeting is opened up for contributions from the floor. Anyone who speaks introduces him/herself by his/her first name only, typically contributors identifying themselves as alcoholic, and offering items from their own experience which overlap with items from the speaker's own story. The speaker will comment on all contributions. Eventually the meeting is closed, often through a reading from the 'Big Book'. The Big Book spells out the 12 steps of recovery on which Alcoholics Anonymous is built, which include 'handing oneself over' to God, as one understands him, and an acceptance of being 'powerless over alcohol'.

Once the formal part of the meeting is completed, members are free to socialise, to continue the process of mutual support by the sharing of common past experiences, or, indeed, by discussion of challenges in the near future such as perceived dangerous drinking situations. Some members receive one-to-one support from a 'sponsor'. A sponsor is usually, but not always, a person with a long period of sobriety behind him/her. The sponsor can generally identify many of the problems, both mental and physical, which new members are experiencing. Long-term dependence on an individual sponsor is, however, discouraged as the main strength is perceived as being in the group.

Separate meetings along similar lines, but managed independently, are held by, and for, the children (Al-Ateen) and the partners (Al-Anon) of problem drinkers.

Central elements in the Alcoholics Anonymous process of helping

Self-disclosure and identification   The meeting places responsibility on individual attenders to recognise and publicly proclaim their own alcoholism through identifying with the experience of others – i.e. 'through having been there too'. This process of sharing experiences with others who offer social acceptance, in spite of what they hear, helps to mitigate against shame, guilt, and stigma. Taking on the new identity of a 'sober alcoholic' offers a means of making sense of these experiences and thus normalising behaviour. By realising that experiences which individual drinkers regarded with either shame or guilt, have been previously experienced by their newfound and sober friends, the goal of becoming a 'sober alcoholic' presents a picture of a future endowed with status and recognition.

Mutual aid   The opportunity to use personal experiences related to drinking to help the new or relapsed participants, allows the member to restructure the meanings attached to their drinking behaviour in a more positive way. Damaged self-esteem can be restored and the welfare value of reciprocity sustained by reminding the new, or relapsed participant of what can happen, as well as serving as a warning against complacency to the 'old guard'. At the same time, the established member is reminded, through helping, of the hazards of active or renewed drinking.

The provision of an alternative way of life   Regular attendance at a Fellowship meeting offers an alternative subculture to that of drinking. For those who have become socially isolated and lack alternative means of support, this is an important social and psychological anchor. For those whose social, familial, or occupational lifestyle imposes heavy drinking pressures, it can be crucial to survival. Attenders are asked to set and achieve new and alternative life goals to maintain abstinence, and only abstinence, basically by living life 'one day at a time', avoiding drinking situations and old drinking companions, and adhering to the ethos of the '12 steps'. Some drinkers experience difficulty in finding the necessary personal and material resources to accept all the implications of what is effectively a new way of life, with no permitted deviations, and are regarded as 'not being ready'. There is no element of choice. AA comes ready-made. It is a package which can either be accepted as it stands, or rejected; there are no compromises or room for negotiation. It is a way of life and in this sense active AA membership can, in the short term, serve as a positive 'cross-addiction', filling the gap left by drinking, until the person is strong enough to lead a less addiction-centred life.

The impact of Alcoholics Anonymous on problem drinkers

In 1979 a major empirical study was carried out by David Robinson which enabled a greater understanding to emerge of the impact of

AA upon drinkers, including some of the concerns experienced by members (Robinson 1976). Robinson's findings underlined the strengths of AA in terms of enabling members to reconstruct their deviant identity, and experience psychological release through publicly 'confessing' drink-related experiences which, however humiliating, could be received as of immense value by someone else. The value of AA was stressed in terms of its immediate accessibility, the compensations offered to the socially isolated and ostracised, and the non-hierarchical structure of the organisation. Not all members were uncritical of their experiences in the fellowship. Indeed, there was active dislike by some attenders of the onus placed upon them to label themselves alcoholic, and to turn themselves over to a 'God'. Sixty-nine per cent of people questioned were unhappy about some aspects of the story-telling, with reference to horrendous tales of drinking episodes told in a somewhat boastful fashion and with little focus on the recovery process.

A concern raised by the research was the impact of the recovery programme on partners and families, many of whom would not have become members of Al-Anon. Regular involvement in the fellowship as a long-term, substitute addiction ran the risk of subordination of family goals and needs to the AA way of life.

Finally, although AA claimed to have been attracting alcoholics at an earlier stage in their drinking careers, this was not borne out by Robinson's findings (Robinson 1979). This underlines a major criticism of the fellowship; which is that people attending who are less damaged by alcohol fail to identify with the anecdotal and sometimes exaggerated experiences reported by members with a much more damaging history of very heavy or dependent drinking. Thus, AA continues to be relevant primarily to dependent drinkers.

The movement towards community-based agencies

The mid 1960s saw the emergence of community-based, specialist alcohol services, most notably Councils on Alcohol, or Alcohol Advisory Services as some are known. In part, this development represented a response to the growing need for services, given the increasing incidence of problem drinking, but also to the redefinition of alcoholism as problem drinking, which can be viewed as a social rather than an exclusively medical problem.

The reorganisation of statutory social work services in the early 1970s when the pervasiveness of alcohol problems within social-work caseloads was beginning to be recognised, facilitated a more direct dialogue between the statutory sector and voluntary agencies specialising in drink problems. Some Social Work and Social

Services Departments, such as that at Strathclyde, addressed the problem at policy level, resulting in the deployment of additional resources for the provision of specialist alcohol information and advice centres (Officers/Members Group Report, Strathclyde Regional Council 1979). Developments within clinical psychology in the study and treatment of addictions helped to reinforce the trend towards community rehabilitation, focusing on the development of behavioural skills in the drinker to identify, resist, and avoid drinking cues. This was followed by the publication in the late 1970s of a series of outcome studies demonstrating the resumption of controlled drinking even by so-called physically dependent drinkers (Heather and Robertson 1981). All this involved a marked shift away from the medical model of alcoholism and a parallel shift away from specialist and institutional services.

Councils on Alcohol/Alcohol Advisory Services

Next to AA, Councils on Alcohol constitute the largest network of services for problem drinkers, within the voluntary sector. They represent a major departure from the disease model. Many clients are helped towards a problem-free drinking pattern (not just abstinence). Personal experience of problem drinking is not considered a prerequisite of helping others. Focal areas for concern include preventative work involving influence on the drinking environment and the availability and price of alcohol itself. There are over 90 regional and local councils in England, Scotland, and Wales. Alcohol Concern (in London) and the Scottish Council on Alcohol (in Glasgow) are the national bodies, relying heavily on central government for financial support. Both bodies have an important role in education and training, and in advising government on policy issues.

Almost all of the local Councils on Alcohol in England and Wales are members of Alcohol Concern, either through a corporate or individual membership, and many other voluntary agencies outwith the council network are in a similar position. As far as councils are concerned, they are generally nominally responsible for the provision of a service in a local authority area. They vary greatly in organisational size, from one local council with almost 50 staff, ranging down to very small councils, based perhaps on a district health authority area, where staff numbers are very limited. Local councils, or Alcohol Advisory Services as many are now called, are perceived as having a range of functions, including a public educational responsibility, providing advice and counselling to people with alcohol problems, providing education and training to specialist workers, developing local preventative strategies, and acting as co-ordinating bodies on alcohol problems within their area.

It is not possible to be specific regarding approaches by Councils on Alcohol to the treatment of problem drinkers in England and Wales. This varies from one area to another, depending upon the philosophy of each organisation. However, it is certainly true to say that it is unusual to find the disease concept regarded as a basis for the problem, or abstinence as the only answer. The development of a range of approaches based on individual needs has been, and is, very noticeable.

Alcohol Concern have a specific remit to help develop new local advisory and counselling services in England and Wales. In the past three years they have provided finance for twelve new services, to which they also provide support and advice in different parts of the country. Alcohol Concern are also interested in providing training and education for statutory services and hold periodic conferences for workers in the statutory sector.

Although autonomous bodies in their own right, all the Scottish local councils are affiliated to The Scottish Council on Alcohol. This enables them to take advantage of an SCA-administered, national scheme, to recruit and train volunteers as alcohol counsellors. There is a common model of service delivery amongst local councils in Scotland, since practice elements such as recording systems, the making of home visits, and procedures for handling employee and court referrals are the subject of a consultative process, through which agreed national guidelines are issued.

There are currently some 400 trainee and accredited voluntary counsellors working in the 25 Councils throughout Scotland. The Councils themselves vary from small rural agencies, run entirely by a voluntary executive committee and other helpers, to large urban organisations employing a mixture of full- and part-time staff. The rigorous, nationally agreed selection scheme through which counsellors are recruited by newspaper advertising, involves a two-stage local and national assessment. This results in around one in four applicants being accepted for training. Acceptability for training depends not on previous personal, or other experience of problem drinking, or educational qualifications, but on the possession of traits and skills which are seen as a prerequisite for personal development as a counsellor. Examples are good listening skills and an absence of rigidity in attitudes and values. Counsellors come from a wide variety of backgrounds, occupations, and social class. Morale amongst voluntary counsellors is high, with very low drop-out rates amongst those who are kept active and well supported. The average 'life' of a voluntary counsellor is between four and five years, during which period most give some 3–4 hours work per week on a regular basis. (Scottish Council on Alcohol and Wilson 1986.)

Basic training, covering six residential weekends or its equivalent, is structured to enable the trainee to develop core counselling skills and a sound understanding of addictive behaviour, with a special focus on alcohol. The counselling model is eclectic, drawing on the humanistic foundations of non-directive counselling (Rogers 1951; Egan 1985), cognitive and behavioural psychology sources, and social work perspectives around values such as confidentiality. More recently, an experiential dimension to training has been introduced, allowing trainees to explore experiences which may be important to practice, such as bereavement, relationship troubles, and drug use.

Training is developed, monitored, and delivered through a national interdisciplinary panel of trainers, with backgrounds in psychology, social work, medicine, and nursing. These area tutors are also managers of local support teams, which provide professional support and supervision for all counsellors working at local level. The support team works closely with any paid staff and with the counselling services subcommittee of the local executive. It is responsible for assessing the development of counsellors' skills and making recommendations on the accreditation of trainees. It also may mount ongoing training from time to time in response to local needs. Glasgow Council on Alcohol, for example, is presently reviewing the need to introduce training on race issues.

Before the introduction of the training scheme in 1979, the service offered to problem drinkers mainly revolved around group counselling often under the directive leadership of a 'recovered' problem drinker, who drew readily on his/her personal experience. Therefore, there were similarities with the AA model. In fact, Glasgow Council on Alcohol was founded by three ex-members of AA who are reputed to have wanted to offer a more flexible style of helping. Today, one-to-one counselling is the norm, with group counselling offered on a selective basis, to meet specific needs. The approach of the alcohol counsellor is holistic and includes involving the partner and other family members whenever possible, as well as working on any problems which impair the wellbeing of the client, such as debt management, sexual problems, family relationships, and other addictions. Counsellors are encouraged also to liaise closely with other agencies, both to undertake joint work and to make appropriate referrals where necessary. Overall, the aim is to enable the client to continue to live in the community and to be able to function competently with alcohol no longer a central feature of their life. Compared with ten years ago, a greater proportion of referrals to local councils are female, are from younger age groups, and are referred from statutory sources such as GPs, social workers, and the courts. The partners of problem drinkers are offered as intensive one-to-one counselling services as are drinkers, and many more are now coming forward. Whilst many of the clients have a long history of dependent drinking and have attended other agencies such as AA in the past, many clients are now presenting for help and advice with what could be regarded as 'early-stage' problems.

In 1987 there were over 4,000 referrals to local councils in Scotland (UK figures are, unfortunately, not available). Sixty-five per cent of those were male, 34 per cent were aged 35 or under, and 47 per cent were in employment. Over the past 10 years, Councils on Alcohol and some other specialist alcohol services have been receiving a steady flow of referrals from employment settings and more recently from the courts through diversion schemes. These new sources of referral have necessitated the setting up of carefully regulated procedures for assessment, monitoring, and reporting.

New sources of referral

Employment referrals

Employers and trade union officials have become increasingly aware of the economic and human costs of problem drinking within the workforce. Employee policies on alcohol abuse, jointly agreed between union and management, have enabled the identification, referral, and support of problem drinkers and their partners to take place. Most referrals to Councils on Alcohol and a few other specialist agencies are made through disciplinary procedures, where work-performance problems have been identified as likely to be alcohol-related. Any disciplinary action is suspended once the employee agrees to attend the local council (or any other designated agency) for assessment and support on the understanding that the agency will report back to the employer about attendance.

It is essential that the employer and the designated agency are able to agree a referral system, which protects against any conflict in the counsellor's accountability to the client, the agency, and the employing organisation. Local councils and the national bodies have been able to collaborate with employers and trade unions in implementing effective policies, particularly through introducing in-service training to assist in the identification of problem drinkers, and education programmes aimed at enabling employees to monitor their own drinking and examine their own need for support. Established 'employee assistance programmes' in Canada and the USA have claimed a high level of effectiveness in that acceptance by the workforce of such schemes has lead to many self-referrals and the recovery of problem drinkers (Hore and Plant 1981).

Court referrals

It is likely that the pioneering work begun by local Councils on Alcohol with young people charged with alcohol-related offences will be given increasing support by statutory bodies and government agencies over future years. The relationship between intoxication and public-order offences has now become a public issue. This work has involved attempts at diverting alcohol-related offenders away from the criminal justice system, not only through the provision of Detoxification Centres and Designated Places (very few such centres, in fact, have been established), but more importantly, through offering the courts an assessment service for problem drinkers and an alcohol-education or counselling facility as part of a deferred sentence 'package'. The whole matter of alcohol-education facilities and diversion schemes is being dealt with in detail by Steve Baldwin in Chapter 3.

It would seem that the threat of disciplinary action in the case of employment referrals, and more severe sentencing in the case of court referrals, serve as a motivating force for the problem drinker, acting as the gateway to the contemplative and action stages of resolving a drinking problem (Prochaska and Diclemente 1983). This is supported by a study comparing different kinds of referral to a local Council on Alcohol, which found that clients referred from hostels and employers had attained the highest rate of compliance.

Some wider issues

Some Councils on Alcohol argue that the fixed cycle of recruiting and training volunteers and the large voluntary teams required to man the urban Councils, create considerable management problems and mitigate against flexibility. In addition, whilst the voluntary sector has been innovative in many respects – the 'Drinkwatchers Programme' pioneered through Accept in London is an example of an attempt at early intervention with less-damaged clients – it has been constrained by resourcing problems and sometimes by resistance to self-monitoring and evaluation (Crawford *et al.* in press). It is notoriously difficult for most voluntary organisations to raise funds – including voluntary alcohol services – indicating that the 'moral' model of problem drinking still prevails in the public mind. Many Councils on Alcohol are in receipt of funding from the alcohol industry itself. It has been argued that this imposes restrictions on their freedom to be vocal with regard to policies concerning the regulation of alcohol in society. Thus the new campaigning body, Action Against Alcohol Abuse, has pledged at its inception never to accept funds, either from the alcohol industry or from Central Government. It has directed its efforts towards social-policy issues such as pricing, availability, advertising, and sponsorship, with a view towards keeping the 'alcohol debate' high in public consciousness.

Councils on Alcohol attempt to combine professional standards of care and accountability with the flexibility and commitment of the voluntary sector. Their development was largely due to the commitment of a small group of individuals who wished to see an alternative to the rigid philosophy of Alcoholics Anonymous. The high profile of the disease model in the 1960s, and its level of acceptance, militated against the development of alternative strategies in the statutory sector. This situation has now changed with a much greater response to alcohol problems from many statutory agencies such as the Social Services Departments in Bradford, Hereford and Worcester, Manchester and Richmond, and the Social Work Department in Strathclyde. The Griffiths Report (1988) recommends the expansion of the Voluntary Sector, but this must be accompanied by a continuation of the increased recognition for intervention in alcohol problems by statutory workers.

Alcohol-related problems are characterised, above all else, by their diversity, so that the emerging variety of community responses is very fitting. However, there are dangers in specialist agencies becoming too isolated from the wider network of services. It is important that both sectors become more conscious of the ways in which they might best link with, and complement, each other's endeavours (Alcohol Concern 1987).

Although specialist community agencies have developed a wide repertoire of helping strategies covering, for example, diversion schemes for drunk drivers, collaborative preventive strategies with health, police, and other agencies, as well as publicity programmes targeted at specific groups such as women and the elderly, they alone cannot deal with the entire range of what is now a very large social problem. Since primary care agents, particularly social workers, community health and psychiatric teams, and GPs very regularly come into contact with problem drinkers, it is essential that they develop the necessary skills of identification, advice, and support, and are able to make appropriate referrals. Hence the need to consider the part to be played by all these professional groups, and especially social workers, in a drive towards the provision of community services.

Further developments in community services

In their 1973 circular while still talking about 'Community Services for Alcoholics' the DHSS acknowledged the need to develop community services for a range of problem drinkers and they also acknowledged an increasing overall awareness of alcohol problems (DHSS 1973). In 1978, the DHSS Advisory Committee, headed by Neil Kessel, reported on 'The Pattern and Range of Services for Problem Drinkers'. This report was based on the assumption that alcohol problems could never be handled by specialist helpers alone. The creation of a sufficient number of specialists to respond directly to problem drinkers and their families was clearly seen as uneconomic and undesirable and the report specifically identified a variety of primary care workers such as social workers, probation officers, GPs, and community-health and psychiatric nurses who 'should be prepared to identify problem drinkers and manage many themselves' (DHSS and Welsh Office 1978).

The report acknowledged there was a need for the adequate training of such primary care workers (this was further addressed in the DHSS Advisory Committee Report on Education and Training in 1979) and recommended that a number of district-based, specialist, multidisciplinary teams should be established to train and support primary care workers.

The Maudsley Alcohol Pilot Project (MAPP) 1973–77

This project was a driving force behind many of the recommendations in the Kessel Report (DHSS and Welsh Office 1978). In 1974, in a general population survey, the MAPP found that the respondents with the heaviest consumption of alcohol and the most severe problems from drinking had relatively frequent contact with primary care workers and yet they received little or no help with their drinking problems (Shaw *et al.* 1978). The MAPP Report suggested that this poor response by primary care workers could be attributed to their anxiety about 'role adequacy', 'role legitimacy', and 'role support'. The workers were anxious because they felt they lacked the information or the skills to recognise and respond to drinking problems; they were unsure whether it was appropriate for them to actually respond and they felt anxious about being unsupported in making any such response. All of these aspects were seen by the MAPP as being caused by inadequate training or deficiencies in the work situation, such as an unsupportive environment.

This work was important in confirming social work practice wisdom about the significance of regular and informed support and supervision. The supervision of practitioners in many local authority Social Service and Social Work Departments is often accorded low priority and assumptions can be made by line managers that only incompetent staff require it. Sometimes staff feel embarrassed about asking for supervision from their line managers, in case it is interpreted as a sign of weakness. Sometimes there is a tendency for staff to rely on an informal system of peer-group support and supervision – more often than not spontaneous discussions about work that may occur with colleagues in staff rooms at lunchtime.

Effective staff are any agency's most valuable resource and the MAPP research indicates quite clearly that if social work staff are to function effectively with problem drinkers, then appropriate support and supervision are vital considerations. What constitutes appropriate support and supervision is an area for further consideration and it seems likely that different staff groups with different levels of experience may benefit from different kinds of support. All staff are likely to benefit from some discussion and 'sharing', but staff who already have some special expertise may benefit from more sophisticated consultation and advice than most line managers, with other numerous concerns, may be able to provide.

The Community Alcohol Team (CAT)

The term Community Alcohol Team was coined by the Maudsley Alcohol Pilot Project in 1975 when the first CAT was established by them on an experimental basis. It was intended to provide primary care workers with the knowledge and the skills necessary to recognise and respond to problem drinkers, to support these workers by offering back-up expertise and advice, and to create a centralised network of resources. Shaw writes:

> The CAT was referred to as a *community* team because its focus of operation was in the community, not in hospitals.

The CAT was called an *alcohol* rather than an alcoholism team because it was attempting to help agents respond to a variety of problems associated with alcohol.

The CAT was called a *team* because it involved agents from different professions. The 2 full-time members were a consultant psychiatrist and a senior social worker.

(Shaw *et al.* 1978: 175)

It was felt that a full-size CAT would probably be most effective on a district basis, perhaps containing a population of 250,000 or so. There are now at least a dozen CATS throughout Great Britain, for example, in Salford, Leicester, Exeter, and Renfrew (Scotland). Often differing in size and approach, many are recently established and there remains a need for more research to monitor and evaluate their effectiveness. Most teams see their main task as a varying combination of direct client work and support of primary workers. Many teams seem to feel they have been pressed into the provision of direct client services and there is a continuing debate about the appropriateness of this.

In this respect a number of CATS have evolved away from the original MAPP model, which emphasised the teaching, training, and support role (second-level interventions) rather than client counselling (first-level interventions). The original MAPP CAT saw the provision of consultation and support as a service for the primary care worker and not the client. It was not thought possible, nor always desirable, for the client to be referred to another agency. In many instances, the client might not wish to go to a specialist agency, having already established a relationship and trust with the primary worker and might not wish to rehearse again details of past history and current trauma to a newcomer. In addition, the client might be less likely to confide openly or readily to a newcomer, until a trusting relationship had been established. From the workers' point of view it was also acknowledged some workers might feel reluctant to have their clients 'taken away' and the consultation service was an offer of a service to the primary worker in order to give support and help to carry on dealing with the client in the community. The MAPP–CAT style of approach aimed to encourage:

the general community agent, who had the most background knowledge and the strongest therapeutic relationship with a client, to maintain the prime therapeutic responsibility for responding to the client's drinking. Yet clients still benefited indirectly from the specialist's expertise and clinical knowledge.

(Shaw *et al.* 1978:248)

The degree to which this model has been accepted and established has varied. Some CATS, such as the one in Renfrew, have accepted that the consultancy service, which has had a consistently poor take-up rate, will now take second place to the provision of in-service training and education. Other CATS record:

> firstly there was the view that the sudden growth of such teams (i.e. CATS) would leave generic workers with 'nothing to do but give out bus passes' and somewhat paradoxically, there was also resentment towards teams offering a consultative service who 'never got their hands dirty'. One Salford social worker commented 'They come in and advise us on how it should be done, that's all very well, but it is us that has to do it! What we need is people who will actually see our clients and do something for them'.
>
> (Clement 1987:126)

The Salford CAT accepted that they needed to be seen as offering more than consultation if the service was to be extensively used. The team agreed to carry out assessments, plus short-term intervention if required, during and after which the primary worker would see the client with CAT support. Some might view this as primary workers taking the easy way out or 'passing the buck!' In writing up the Salford Experiment, Clement described it as a shift 'from advising workers on good practice to actually modelling that good practice' (Clement 1987:126). In the Salford Experiment, only the probation officers, who clearly saw working with problem drinkers as relevant and a priority in terms of agency remit, felt that their line managers assigned a high degree of priority to working with problem drinkers, and were thus more likely to use the CAT in a consultative fashion.

Other CATS have experienced difficulties with the task of education and training. GPs have consistently been a difficult group to reach in this way. The evaluation of the Salford CAT states: 'the question of the best way to input training to GPs remained unresolved during the period of project evaluation' (Clement 1987:128). Other CATS have debated whether multidisciplinary or unidisciplinary training is the right course.

Ultimately the Salford findings reinforce the MAPP emphasis on the importance of providing both support and training for workers. They also show, however, that the provision of role support to the worker has to come from the worker's line manager before the benefits of an external consultancy service will have any real effect: 'In the absence of support from management in working with drinkers in those cases where alcohol problems are being identified, the consultative role of the CAT will become minimised' (Clement 1987:142). Cartwright (1980) has already shown that training without effective role support will not increase the involvement of workers with problem drinkers. Clearly, then, how to provide for, and improve upon, the internal provision of role support to primary care workers is a factor to merit priority attention. Clement (1987) concludes the problem was ultimately not that of the 'therapeutically uncommitted agent' but, ironically, that of the 'therapeutically uncommitted agency'. Lack of political will at both local and central government level and ultimately lack of resources were seen as major obstacles to implementing a truly community-based response at primary care level. A number of other factors are also significant here and should be considered.

The role for pre-qualification and in-service training

In order for helping professionals such as social workers, probation officers, nurses, and health visitors to identify and work with problem drinkers, they must acknowledge the need for this and be willing and able to do so. The development of alcohol education as part of pre-qualifying education and in-service training could go some way towards this and the CAT appears to have a proven contribution to make in the latter connection. Each primary care agency or relevant profession should review the adequacy of existing training arrangements. Some workers, such as social workers, fail to recognise the applicability or transferability of their existing skills in working with problem drinkers. In addition some of the 'traditional' social work values such as acceptance and self-determination can get in the way of the social worker's ability to assess and intervene in drinking patterns (Collins *et al.* 1988). Such issues may require particular attention (see also Chapter 2).

The organisational framework

To place all the emphasis on primary care workers' knowledge and skills ignores the organisational framework in which they function. If, as previously stated, the low priority attached by many agencies to working with problem drinkers is due to a lack of political will at local and central government level and a lack of resources, this may mean that such agencies are so overworked that they are struggling to carry out even a basic operational service. Yet there is an accumulating wealth of evidence to suggest that the consequences of alcohol misuse contribute greatly to social workers' caseloads, while social work agencies still do not regard alcohol problems as a high-priority concern. Working with problem drinkers and their families needs to be acknowledged and sanctioned by agency managers and there are significant organisational issues to be addressed. The Social Work Service Group Practice Guidance points out that in the past much has been left to the individual enthusiasms of practitioners in developing services for problem drinkers, but this has all too often occurred without formal authority and it has been all too easy for such developments to be abandoned when the individual practitioner moves on. The guidance states:

> The development of effective social work service is dependent on the agency establishing:
> a. a clearly worked out policy statement which legitimates alcohol problems as a focus of attention and encourages innovative practice;
> b. an approach on the part of managers that enables practitioners to give time, and to apply the relevant skills, to the prevention and the resolution of alcohol problems among their clients.
> (Social Work Services Group 1988:36)

It may be that more research is needed which is specifically directed at the impact of alcohol misuse on the resources of primary care staff and agencies to convince management that working with problem drinkers is relevant as a priority agency function. It may be that managers themselves need to be the first target in terms of raising their awareness of the issue and that top-level negotiations need to be made to effect change, as clearly a 'bottom-up' approach is causing difficulties.

A planned approach in working with problem drinkers

As we have emphasised already, the case for a broadly based, co-ordinated, multidisciplinary response to alcohol problems seems clear – people with alcohol problems are many and varied and they will be encountered in a variety of settings with a variety of different presenting problems. It is suggested that working with problem drinkers should remain the responsibility of primary care agencies, such as Social Services and Social Work Departments, health centres, and Probation Services, and that as they will be dealing with the majority of problem drinkers, they will require appropriate support and training. It is suggested also that there is still a role for specialised services for the treatment of some patients (e.g. special NHS units). Overall attention is then required to planning services at a regional level. It seems unrealistic to expect in the immediate future that resources will be anything but scarce and attention needs to be given to developing a truly collaborative approach, which leads to the effective use of existing resources. This needs to occur at regional and area level, based on relevant demographic considerations, appropriate statistics, and individual and collective practice experience. Without effective collaboration, clients will receive an uncoordinated and discontinuous approach which they may manipulate to great effect, if they wish to avoid seriously confronting the difficulties caused by their drinking.

It is recognised that real pressures upon agency staff at all levels may mitigate against collaboration. Staff may find it easier to work within the confines of their own agency ethos rather than trying to work across agency boundaries and may unwittingly collude with evasive behaviour by a client. Different professional values and different professional cultures complicate interagency policy negotiations and practice issues. Collaboration also takes time and a seemingly endless round of meetings. The desire to just pass a client onto someone, 'an expert' in that particular field, will seem a tempting solution to a hard-pressed social worker struggling to keep all their appointments for that day. It is ironic to find that social workers who may have spent 2 years or more training for their professional qualification refer and defer to a 'specialist' voluntary worker in a Council on Alcohol who may have only spent the equivalent of 12 days on their training course. This is not to suggest that such a referral is inappropriate or irrelevant. Many clients will find the approach of the volunteer beneficial; volunteers often have more time, they often have considerable life experience, and, after some years of practice, many will have acquired specialist skills and knowledge. What seems important is that any referral by a primary care worker should have been thought through, with its implications discussed by both worker and client prior to referral. Any referral should be part of a planned approach in working with a problem drinker – not just a question of 'passing the buck' because time is pressing.

Sometimes collaboration does not take place because workers will fail to recognise the alcohol problem at all, so intent will they be on dealing with the presenting problems that seem most relevant to the overall remit of their own agencies. It is suggested that all primary care workers, whatever their agency and the client's presenting problem, should be aware of the high incidence of alcohol-related problems in the general population and initial assessments should always include questions relating to alcohol consumption. (For more details on this the reader is referred to Chapters 2 and 3.) Sometimes collaboration can seem to become an end in itself and an excuse to delay or defer painful decision-making. Painful because shared action and shared resources means giving as well as receiving. If collaboration is to work, we also need to develop relationships of trust as well as keeping a firm eye on the ultimate goal – the welfare of the client, not the organisation.

Future developments

Recent years have seen the promotion of community-orientated mental health programmes and it is arguable that community mental health centres or teams may soon exist on similar lines to the CAT. The most recent debate relating to the CAT centres on whether CATs should combine with Community Drug Teams (CDTs) and as there is evidence of the medical model losing general credibility and a shifting emphasis towards recognition of the psychological commonalities of addictive behaviours, it is but a short step from there to CDTs combining with community health teams (Hebblethwaite 1988). The Advisory Council on the Misuse of Drugs in their treatment and rehabilitation report in 1982 recommended extending the network of agencies likely to become involved with problem drug takers. They said: 'services in the future need to be geared to solve common problems rather than being merely substance or diagnosis centred' and would thus seem to be giving clear guidance towards the adoption of a commonality approach (DHSS 1982).

Certainly there might be a number of positive benefits accruing from such a move. For instance, at the moment it is commonplace for workers who are competent in working with clients in one area to feel deskilled when working with clients in another area. The difficulty social workers experience in recognising the relevance of some of their traditional social work skills and methods has already been mentioned earlier in the chapter. Recognition of commonalities might demystify myths surrounding various types of drug use and behaviours, thus allowing for the easier recognition of transferable skills. It is also arguable that a common approach would enable maximum use of existing resources in education, training, service provision, and research – thus avoiding time-consuming competition and possible duplication.

Arguments against such an approach suggest that people with alcohol problems, those with drug problems, and those with mental health problems are different groups reflecting different needs and different problems. As such, a common approach could be seen as a disservice.

Given the evidence cited in the Advisory Council report in 1982 that most drug users are not exclusive users of one drug, but are multiple drug users, it is perhaps easier to accept Community Alcohol Teams becoming Community Addiction Teams than to see the latter combining with community health teams. It has taken some years and fierce debate to shift the helping of problem drinkers away from the dominance of the disease model. Until community mental health centres can demonstrate the reality of a community care approach, which offers a genuine alternative to hospital treatment and 'less emphasis on disease and more on problems of living' (Hebblethwaite 1988:27), any centre which promotes a common problem approach may well be treated with suspicion.

In conclusion, in the latter half of this chapter, we have examined recent developments in the provision of community services for problem drinkers. We have considered the helping contributions of organisations such as Alcoholics Anonymous and Councils on Alcohol and, more recently, the growth of Community Alcohol Teams. We have explored organisational perspectives at national, regional, and local levels, which are clearly significant in the delivery of such services. In the next chapter we will move on and specifically consider the prevalence of alcohol abuse in the caseloads of statutory social workers, the role of statutory social work in providing help to those with alcohol-related problems, and the difficulties which workers experience in supplying such help. We shall emphasise and elaborate on the knowledge and skills that social workers already possess which can be built upon to develop confidence when intervening with alcohol-related problems – provided effective support is made available from within the hierarchy of statutory agencies.

© 1990 Stewart Collins, Gill Ottley, and Mary Wilson

References

Alcohol Concern (1987) *Alcohol Services. The Future*, Cambridge: Woodhead-Faulkner.

Armor, D., Pollich, J., and Stambul, M. (1978) *Alcoholism and Treatment*, New York: Wiley.

Cahalan, D. (1970) *Problem Drinkers: A National Survey*, San Francisco: Jossey-Bass.

Cartwright, A. (1980) 'The attitudes of helping agents towards the alcoholic client: the influence of experience, support, training and self-esteem', *British Journal of Addiction* 75:413–31.

Clement, S. (1987) 'The Salford Experiment: an account of the Community Alcohol Team approach', in T. Stockwell and S. Clement (eds) *Helping the Problem Drinker: New Initiatives in Community Care*, London: Croom Helm.

Collins, S., Ottley, G., and Wilson, M. (1988) 'Counselling problem drinkers and social work education in Scotland, *Social Work Education* 7(3):17–24.

Crawford, A., Robertson, I., *et al.* (in press) 'Drinkwatchers in Scotland: Pilot Early Intervention Study', *Journal of Alcohol and Addiction*.

Davis, A.M. (1989) *Pssst . . . A Really Useful Guide to Alcohol*, London: Pan.

DHSS (1973) *Community Services for Alcoholics*, DHSS Circular 21/73, London: HMSO.

DHSS and Welsh Office (1978) *The Pattern and Range of Services for Problem Drinkers*, Report by the Advisory Committee on Alcoholism, London: HMSO.

DHSS and Welsh Office (1979) *Report on Education and Training*, Report by the Advisory Committee on Alcoholism, London: HMSO.

DHSS (1981) *Drinking Sensibly*, London: HMSO.

DHSS (1982) *Treatment and Rehabilitation*, Report of the Advisory Council on the Misuse of Drugs, London: HMSO.

Dorn, N. (1983) *Alcohol, Youth and the State*, London: Croom Helm.

Egan, G. (1985) *The Skilled Helper: A Systematic Approach to Effective Helping*, Monterey: Brooks Cole.

Gusfield, J. (1963) *Symbolic Crusade*, Illinois: University of Illinois Press.

Harrison, B. (1971) *Drink and the Victorians*, London: Faber and Faber.

Hawkins, K. and Pass, C. (1979) *The Brewing Industry*, London: Heinemann.

Heather, N. and Robertson, I. (1981) *Controlled Drinking*, London: Methuen.

Heather, N. and Robertson, I. (1985) *Problem Drinking: The New Approach*, Harmondsworth: Penguin.

Hebblethwaite, D. (1988) 'Community Mental Health Centres – a new service for addictions', *New Directions in the Study of Alcohol Group*, Members Booklet, Number Fourteen, May.

Hore, B. and Plant, M. (eds) (1981) *Alcohol Problems in Employment*, London: Croom Helm.

Jeffs, B. and Saunders, W. (1983) 'Minimising alcohol related offences by enforcement of existing licensing legislation', *British Journal of Addiction* 78:67–77.

Jellinek, E.M. (1960) *The Disease Concept of Alcoholism*, New Haven: Hillhouse Press.

Levine, M. (1978) 'The discovery of addiction: changing conceptions of habitual drunkenness in America', *Journal of Studies of Alcohol* 39:143–74.

Mathias, P. (1979) *The Transformation of England*, London: Methuen.

Mello, N. and Mendelson, J. (1965) 'Operant analysis of drinking habits of chronic alcoholics', *Nature* 206:43–6.

Mello, N., McNamee, H., and Mendelson, J. (1968) 'Drinking patterns of chronic alcoholics: gambling and motivation for alcohol', *Psychiatric Research* (24) Washington APA.

Orford, J. (1985) *Excessive Appetites: A Psychological View of Addictions*, London: John Wiley.

Plant, M.A. (1979) *Drinking Careers: Occupations, Drinking Habits and Drinking Problems*, London: Tavistock Publications.

Plant, M.L. (1986) 'Drinking in pregnancy and fetal harm: results from a Scottish prospective study', *Midwifery* 2:81–5.

Pollich, J., Armor, D., and Braiker, H. (1980) *The Course of Alcoholism: Four Years After Treatment*, Santa Monica: Rand Corporation.

Prochaska, J.O. and Diclemente, C.C. (1983) 'Stages and processes of self-change in smoking – towards an integrative mode of change', *Journal of Consulting and Clinical Psychology* 51(3):390–5.

Quinn, M. and Johnstone, R. (1976) 'Alcohol problems in acute male medical admissions', *Health Bulletin* 34:253.

Robinson, D. (1976) *From Drinking to Alcoholism*, Chichester: John Wiley.

Rogers, C.R. (1951) *Client Centred Therapy*, Boston: Houghton Mifflin.

Roizen, R., Cahalan, D., and Shanks, P. (1978) 'Spontaneous remission amongst untreated problem drinkers', in D. Kandel (ed.) *Longitudinal Research on Drug Use*, New York: Wiley.

Room, R. (1984) 'Sociology and the disease concept of alcoholism', in R. Gibbons *et al.* (eds) *Research Advances in Alcohol and Drug Problems* 7, London: Plenum Press.

Royal College of Psychiatrists (1986) *Alcohol: Our Favourite Drug*, London: Tavistock.

Saunders, W. (1984) 'Alcohol use in Britain: how much is too much?' *Health Education Journal* 43(2, 3):66–70.

Saunders, W. and Allsop, S. (1985) 'Giving up addictions', in F. Watts (ed.) *New Developments in Clinical Psychology*, Chichester: British Psychological Society in association with John Wiley Ltd.

Saunders, W. and Kershaw, P. (1979) 'Spontaneous remission from alcoholism: results from a community survey', *British Journal of Addiction* 74:251–65.

Scottish Council on Alcohol and Wilson, M. (1986) 'Counsellor drop out and retention – a research study into the relationship between voluntary counsellor retention, the quality of supervision and other factors', Glasgow: unpublished paper.

Scottish Health Education Co-Ordinating Committee (1985) *A Report on Health Education in the Prevention of Alcohol-related Problems*, Edinburgh: Scottish Health Education Group.

Shaw, S., Cartwright, A., Spratley, T., and Harwin, J. (1978) *Responding to Drinking Problems*, London: Croom Helm.

Sobell, M. and Sobell, L. (1978) *Behavioural Treatment of Alcohol Problems*, New York: Plenum Press.

Social Work Services Group (1988) *SWSG Practice Guidance Towards Effective Practice with Problem Drinkers*, Edinburgh: Scottish Education Department.

Spring, J. and Buss, D. (1977) 'Three centuries of alcohol in the British Diet', *Nature* 270:567–72.

Strathclyde Regional Council Officers/Members Group Report (1979) *Addiction: Collusion or Cover Up?* Glasgow: Strathclyde Regional Council Social Work Department.

Taylor, D. (1981) *Alcohol Reducing the Harm*, London: Office of Health Economics.

Thorley, A. (1985) 'The limitations of the alcohol dependence syndrome in multi-disciplinary service development', in N. Heather, I. Robertson, and P. Davis (eds) *The Misuse of Alcohol: Crucial Issues in Dependence Treatment and Prevention*, London: Croom Helm.

Tuchfeld, B. (1976) *Changes in Patterns of Alcohol Use Without Aid of Formal Treatment*, N. Carolina: Center for Health Studies Research Triangle Institute.

Vaillant, G. (1983) *The Natural History of Alcoholism*, London: Harvard University Press.

Williams, P. and Brake, J. (1980) *Drink in Great Britain 1900–1979*, London: Edsel.

Chapter two

Social work and alcohol

Tom Leckie

It is impossible for social work to ignore alcohol completely. Alcohol is an integral part of our society, and the problems associated with it impinge significantly on the operations of social workers. Yet social work's response has been less than energetic, often fragmented, and frequently uncoordinated. It has been left to a few motivated individuals to highlight the issue within the profession, and a few authorities to respond in a meaningful way by means of policy, resource provision, training, and support.

Prevalence

In the past decade, several studies have indicated the significant prevalence of alcohol abuse in social workers' caseloads. In 1979, a study in Glasgow of 351 active family cases reported that 25 per cent of the caseloads of social workers had alcohol-related problems (McGarva 1979). In 1980 in Lothian a smaller study of 43 current family cases in one urban housing estate reported alcohol-related problems in 40 per cent of the cases (Osborn and Leckie 1980). While a few years later, an Avon study, using a questionnaire based on the Lothian material, found that of 250 active family cases in the Social Services Department, 20 per cent had alcohol-related problems (Abel 1983).

The differences in the findings, might in part be accounted for by the sizes of the samples, the difficulties in defining alcohol-related problems, and the different geographical areas, which might have a significant variation in the general alcohol-related problems reported. Yet another factor was that in the Lothian study, the social workers were given a short training course in alcohol problems prior to the research being undertaken. Training was seen as important in the Lothian study to counteract the problems social workers were identified as having in relation to recognition of clients with alcohol problems in the Maudsley Alcohol Project (Shaw *et al.* 1978).

The problems of social workers

Social workers have a number of difficulties in identifying, engaging, and working with clients with alcohol problems, not all of them rational. As members of a culture which accepts alcohol as its drug of choice, but portrays an ambivalent attitude to its use, and to some extent to its overuse, social workers will bring into their professional work feelings, experiences, attitudes, prejudices, and much ignorance, all of which will have an impact on their work. At one extreme, there will be a small minority of social workers who themselves experience alcohol problems; one estimate is that between 3 and 6 per cent of all social workers employed in Britain have serious alcohol problems (Fanti 1987). This small minority will almost inevitably have great difficulty in identifying and working with those with alcohol problems. This minority will consist of workers at all levels in the organisation, thus influencing not only practice, but also supervision, management, training, and policy.

But there are more general, and widespread problems. One is the acceptance of myths about alcoholism, and the carrying of stereotypes of 'alcoholics', despite the movement away from such models in the last few years (see Chapter 1). So, some social workers continue to hold on to the stereotypes of the alcoholic as being 'ill' and therefore in need of help that is not the province of the social worker, but that of the doctor; as being 'not motivated' and therefore 'difficult, if not impossible, to help'; as being aggressive and potentially dangerous; as being 'down and out'; as being 'devious', 'manipulative', and 'unpredictable'. These beliefs, in some instances might have some foundation. People who drink heavily can be very seriously physically ill and in need of medical intervention, but the model outlined in Chapter 1 clearly illustrates that physical harm and medical intervention are only part of a more complex set of problems, and only apply to *some* drinkers. Many problem drinkers do not seem to be as keen to do something about their own drinking as others are for them to do something. However, Miller's (1983) work on motivational interviewing points out that this does not exclude help being successful, particularly if the counsellor recognises the ambivalence anyone has about changing drinking behaviour, and has the appropriate skills at his/her disposal to help (see Chapter 3). Some problem drinkers can be aggressive, but this is true of other social-work clients, and many agencies are producing or have produced guidelines on how to respond to potential violence; some do indeed become 'habitual drunken offenders', but that only applies to approximately 2 per cent of those who have alcohol problems (Royal College of Psychiatrists 1979). No doubt some problem drinkers are devious, manipulative, and unpredictable, but as yet no study to my knowledge has proven that they are much more or less so than other clients who are recipients of social work services.

Although these myths can be refuted, and the stereotypes shown to be erroneous, the results of social workers holding these beliefs are serious for the clients with drink problems who come into contact with the Probation Services, Social Services, and Social Work Departments. Either (a) nothing is done about the drinking problem – Leckie and his co-workers noted that 'on the whole, the drink problem, even when identified as such, was not tackled' (Leckie *et al.* 1984:16), or (b) the relatives of the problem drinker might be supported, but the responsibility for helping the problem drinker was felt to rest with other services (Isaacs and Moon 1985).

Unfortunately, the failure to respond appropriately after recognition of an alcohol problem is not the most serious deficiency in the social work response. Although there is a dearth of research in this area, and this in itself is perhaps significant, it is likely that social workers fail even to recognise that many of their clients have alcohol problems at all. Leckie *et al.* noted that the high level of cases recognised in the Lothian survey (after a short training course) contrasted with the low figure in official statistics of about 5 or 6 per cent. Shaw *et al.* had identified that 'hidden', i.e. unrecognised, problem drinkers do take their problem to nonspecialist agencies in the community, such as social work offices, but that usually 'the subject of drinking was never brought up by the client, and was never recognised by the agent' (Shaw *et al.* 1978:124). This is a sorry picture. But why has it come about?

There are various reasons why clients do not present their problems as being due to drinking, such as ignorance about the part alcohol plays in the difficulties they are having; uncertainty about who might help; guilt or shame which might prevent an open discussion of all the facts surrounding a problem. And, interestingly, Shaw and his co-workers found that many clients did not feel that it was appropriate to talk to a social worker about drinking. Of their sample, 59 per cent thought that social workers had the right to ask about drinking, while 41 per cent (72 respondents) felt that social workers never had the right to ask clients about their drinking. Table 2.1 clarifies the reasons given. So clients may not bring their problem drinking to social workers for discussion.

Tom Leckie

Table 2.1 Reasons given by clients for not discussing drinking with a social worker

Reasons	Number of respondents
1. The client's drinking is his private concern	23
2. It is not part of the social worker's function	17
3. A social worker has not got the right or authority	13
4. A social worker is not qualified enough	12
5. A social worker has no medical understanding	7

Source: Shaw *et al.* 1978:126.

But this does not relieve statutory Social Services of the responsibility to help those with alcohol problems.

Education and training

Some of the responsibility for this failure by social workers to recognise and respond appropriately to alcohol problems in their caseloads must be put at the door of social work education – or lack of education. The Lothian study (Osborne and Leckie 1980) found that basic training courses rarely considered the knowledge and skills required to intervene effectively in alcohol problems. In the Avon study (Abel 1983) almost half the social workers completing a questionnaire had no input on alcohol problems on their training courses and, since qualifying, 80 per cent had not attended any training courses in developing their skills in intervening in situations where alcohol-related problems were evident. Isaacs and Moon (1985) found in Hampshire that 'a large majority of interviewees (28 out of 40) considered they had 'no specific training at all' on alcohol use and misuse. Therefore, many social workers still leave training courses with no training in helping clients who misuse alcohol; this despite the fact that when asked, social workers commonly report experience of working with clients with alcohol-related problems – in Isaacs and Moon's study 39 out of 40 workers said they had such experience, and 32 out of 40 said they had clients on their caseload at present with alcohol problems. In the Lothian study, all 19 social workers said they had at least one client with a definite alcohol problem.

Those involved in providing both qualifying and in-service training have their problems, which are similar to those who work in front-line agencies – they, too, have had little training in helping those with alcohol problems, and have therefore little confidence in training others. This difficulty is exacerbated by the fact that knowledge and skills in the field advance rapidly, and it is difficult to

46

keep up. This can mean that training, where it has been given, might have been excessively focused upon psychodynamic approaches or upon broader systems thinking which may encourage the worker to make excessive use of other agencies. Furthermore, CCETSW have given no firm directions as to whether every social work course should have input on alcohol problems; the length of such input; and the content of it. The result of all of this is that the interest and commitment of individual educators and groups of students determine whether alcohol problems appear on a training course, the length of the input, and the nature of it (Collins *et al.* 1988).

This is a particularly frustrating situation as what is required to produce social workers competent in dealing with alcohol problems is not excessively complicated. The contents of existing social work training should equip practitioners with a foundation of the basic skills and knowledge required. Tether and Robinson suggest that what is needed beyond that is:

> specific knowledge about the nature and range of alcohol related problems, an understanding of the role which alcohol can play in the cases with which social workers are routinely called upon to deal and the confidence to identify and respond to the alcohol component of those cases.
>
> (Tether and Robinson 1986:229)

At present, social workers often leave training courses to work in Probation, Social Services, and Social Work Departments ill-prepared to deal with the problems surrounding the misuse of alcohol, despite the fact that, when asked, the vast majority recognise that they have problem drinkers on their caseloads.

Training, of course, does not stop on qualification, and statutory social work agencies have a responsibility to ensure that those working for them have further, additional training to supplement basic training. Unfortunately, initiatives such as in-service training courses on alcohol problems, and the sending of appropriate staff to external courses are fragmentary.

There are, however, some important training initiatives which are attempting to redress this situation. The Scottish Council on Alcohol, with support from CCETSW, are developing a training pack for use by social work educators. Specialist alcohol centres like those at Paisley College and at the University of Kent offer post-qualifying courses of varying lengths to enable some social workers to develop their skills; and some social work agencies do run in-service training courses in alcohol problems. The Social Work Services Group in Scotland recently issued a Practice Guidance booklet entitled *Towards Effective Practice With*

Problem Drinkers, in which several simple actions to alleviate the situation in the short term are suggested (Social Work Services Group 1988). They include encouraging those working on qualifying courses to include in their teaching examples the circumstances in which alcohol problems occur; specialised fieldwork placements in alcohol agencies for those students particularly interested in the topic; and the provision of opportunities to work with problem drinkers in area teams and residential and day-care settings. However, much more needs to be accomplished in training, by CCETSW, by individual courses, and by statutory agencies to prepare social workers to respond effectively to the misuse of the most widely used psychoactive drug in this country.

Lest those who are responsible for training think that they have been unfairly singled out for criticism, let me quickly make clear that the training issue is only one link in a process of neglect by social work in the field of alcohol problems. This process was highlighted by Leckie *et al.* (1984:17) as a 'Vicious Circle' (see Figure 2.1).

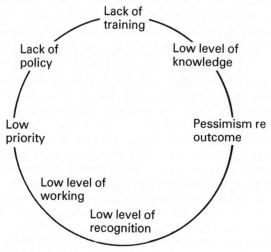

Source: Leckie *et al.* 1984.

Note: Little training leads to a low level of knowledge and pessimism about the outcome of intervention. This leads to a low level of recognition and a low level of working with the problems; which means that the problem has a low level of priority, with often no specific policy on alcohol problems. Hence a low level of training is given.

Figure 2.1   Diagram of a vicious circle

Confidence

It is clear then, that social workers in general feel that they leave training courses with little or no knowledge and uncertain skills about working with alcohol problems. This inevitably leads to what Shaw and his colleagues described as 'anxieties about role adequacy' (Shaw *et al.* 1978:130). Included in this were inability to recognise clues about problem drinking, failure to detect drinking problems, and a sense of hopelessness. In a study by Fanti in 1985 of field social workers' attitudes to problem drinkers in Hereford and Worcestershire, 51 per cent of the social workers interviewed felt that they lacked sufficient skills and knowledge to work effectively with this group (Fanti 1985a). And in a 1981 study by Goodman in Newcastle, 72 per cent of those interviewed did not feel they knew how to counsel problem drinkers in the long term (Goodman 1981).

Shaw and his colleagues also identified a problem which they termed 'anxieties about role legitimacy' (Shaw *et al.* 1978:136), i.e. uncertainty about whether social workers have the right to discuss drinking with their clients. Shaw found that in 1978, over one-third of social workers interviewed disagreed with the statement 'social workers have the right to ask any client how much they drink', and others were uncertain. Fanti in 1985, however, found that 80 per cent of the social workers in his study felt they had the right to comment on a client's drinking (Fanti 1985a). Obviously, this is a confusing issue for social workers. The uncertainty in Shaw *et al.*'s study came, according to the social workers interviewed, from confusion about the lack of statutory obligation to help, and their perception of drinking problems being deemed a low priority by departmental policy. These difficulties were further compounded by an observed lack of 'role support'. This lack of support referred to the perceived need for specialists in alcohol problems in their own organisations (supported by 71 per cent of social workers), scepticism about the effectiveness of specialist agencies, the lack of good co-operation among community agencies, and the subsequent feelings of 'operating in a vacuum . . . without any worthwhile assistance from others' (Shaw *et al.* 1978:142).

It is hardly surprising, in the light of all this, that social workers fail to recognise and work with problem drinkers, especially since few clients come to Social Services Departments specifically for help with alcohol problems; presenting problems instead associated with child care, debt, housing, offending, or family relationships. Drink may be a hidden problem, and one which, as Abel identifies, neither the client nor the client's family offer information about, and the social worker fails to investigate (Abel 1983). However, Abel identifies 'direct indicators of alcohol abuse' reported by the social workers in his study (see Table 2.2). To offer effective help, therefore, two things are necessary. First, social workers must be able to identify signs of alcohol abuse. Second, they must have the confidence in their knowledge and skills to help the client with his/her alcohol abuse, as without this it is often difficult for other problems, sometimes serious ones, to be resolved.

Table 2.2 Direct indicators of alcohol abuse

Indicator	No. of cases	Percentage
1. Social workers observation of intoxication	19	45
2. Alcohol-related offences	16	38
3. Reportage by spouse	14	33
4. Reportage by other professionals/agencies	13	31
5. Smelling of drink	10	24
6. Reportage by others in the family	6	14
7. Reportage by drinkers themselves	4	9
8. Observation of hand tremors/sweating etc. (e.g. withdrawal)	3	7

Source: Abel 1983.

Client groups

A review of research into different client groups within social work and the place of alcohol problems in each group highlights the importance of identifying alcohol problems where they exist, and of being able to work with clients with alcohol problems. In recent years, for instance, there is a growing body of research highlighting a connection between alcohol problems and child care.

Children

The Lothian research, and that of Abel in Avon, indicated clearly that alcohol problems existed in current family cases; that multiple problems were noted in these families, and that the majority of the cases were long standing. They also noted a high level of statutory involvement (see Table 2.3). Apart from the studies in Lothian and Avon, a number of recent studies in Great Britain have suggested that alcohol plays a significant part, or is a significant feature, in families where child abuse is suspected (McGarva 1979; Oliver 1985; Creighton 1976; Behling 1979; Orford *et al.* 1984). Parents under the influence of drink or drugs and unable to exercise proper

Table 2.3   The existence of alcohol problems in family cases

	Lothian (1980) %	Avon (1983) %
Statutory involvement	52	42
Case open 1 year +	76	68
Case open 2 years +	52	52
Intention to close in 3 months	29	36
Child 'at risk'	53	68
RIC – current/previous	47	42

Source: Leckie 1980; Abel 1983.

care was the largest single reason for the reception of children into care by the Social Work Department Standby Service in one region between 1 January and 31 August 1981 (Strathclyde Regional Council 1981). And a Newcastle Social Services Department study found alcohol abuse to be the greatest single factor influencing the number of children aged under 10 in care, and a significant factor in the over-10s (Newcastle City Council Social Services Department Policy Division 1987).

Birleson and Whigmore's and BASW's policy guidelines point out that because of problems of methodology, and definitions of alcohol abuse, we have to be careful not to assume that: 'drug abuse is synonymous with child abuse' (Birleson and Whigmore 1987) and that: 'No clear research association has been made between alcohol use in families and the presentation to social work services of child abuse and neglect' (BASW 1989). However, alcohol abuse can be seen at least to be a prominent feature in child-care work. Birleson and Whigmore stress the need for good assessment, and applaud the decision by Newcastle Social Services to include a 'substance slot' in all future training in child abuse. They urge other statutory Social Services and Social Work Departments and social work courses to do the same. Although, then, the exact place of alcohol abuse in child abuse is unclear, what is clear is that in the present climate on child abuse, we cannot afford to neglect the part alcohol plays.

Offenders

Although the link with child care is an important one for social work agencies, alcohol abuse is an issue in other aspects. Alcohol also has a significant part to play in work with offenders, although there is perhaps not the volume of research that there is in the field of child care. Recent British studies have shown that a significant number of offences are committed while the person is intoxicated (Bennett and Wright 1984; Myers 1982; Jeffs and Saunders 1983).

Gloucester Probation Service in 1984, found alcohol to be involved in the commission of 78 per cent of assaults, 80 per cent of breaches of the peace, 88 per cent of cases of criminal damage, and 33 per cent of child abuse cases. Perhaps more significantly for social work, they found that alcohol abuse featured in 22.5 per cent of all social inquiry reports in the same year (Gloucester Probation Service 1984). A Lothian study of social inquiry reports found that at least 50 per cent of offences were thought to be alcohol-related, while another Scottish study found alcohol to be an important factor in 17 per cent of social inquiry reports. (Dickie 1985; Curran and Chambers 1982). Yet another British study would suggest that Curran and Chambers' figures may underestimate the size of the problem, as it found that only limited attention was given to the role of alcohol when preparing a report 'even in cases where large amounts of alcohol had been consumed prior to commission of the offence' (Coope 1979:23). Despite these figures, Scottish statistics indicated that in 1981, only about 1 per cent of cases involving breach of the peace, drunkenness, and drunk driving were given probation. Most of those who offended in these categories were dealt with by fines (Scottish Home and Health Department 1981).

In recent years, some statutory social services have become involved with offenders with alcohol-related problems by setting up various schemes diverting offenders from custodial sentences (Collins and Tate 1988). This type of intervention by social workers and probation officers is developing throughout Britain, and it may be an area of work of growing importance in the future (see also Chapter 3).

Older people

A group which has had some publicity recently in relation to their drinking problems is older people. The concern has been highlighted by Age Concern and Age Concern Scotland, who have issued leaflets on 'Older People and Alcohol' to stress the dangers and offer clear and useful advice to clients and professionals. Older people are particularly at risk from harm from alcohol for a number of reasons, e.g. some use alcohol to numb the pain of loss. Also, alcohol does not mix well with some prescribed medication, and older people are more liable to be taking various cocktails of prescribed medication. Older people who are finding it difficult to cope are a particular responsibility of, and a particular concern to

Social Work and Social Services departments, and there is a small but growing number of studies which help to identify the extent of the problems related to alcohol among this group. A study by Longman of 50 home-help clients in a London borough revealed that 28 per cent asked for drink to be bought for them on a weekly basis, and half of these consumed up to three bottles of spirits per week (Longman 1985). Also, Fanti conducted a small survey of elderly people receiving regular home-help service, which gave cause for concern in that he found that 12 per cent drank every day (Fanti 1985). Most worrying of all, in a recent study by Goodman it was shown that as many a 20 per cent of elderly people admitted to a geriatric hospital were admitted as a direct result of alcohol abuse (Goodman 1984).

Of particular relevance to social work is an opinion reached by Zimberg, that help for older people with alcohol problems is best provided not in specialist alcohol settings, but by agencies and in settings which are used to helping older people, and should include the possibility of help in the person's home (Zimberg 1978).

Ethnic minorities

There have been few studies on alcohol problems among ethnic minorities. One in Manchester and Liverpool suggested that between 2.8 and 3.7 per cent of the Asian population there had alcohol problems (Ghosh 1984). According to BASW's document on Policy Guidelines, 'a number of agencies are beginning to look at the particular needs of ethnic minorities and see how they can best be met' (BASW 1989). It advises Social Work and Social Services Departments that their workers should be aware of possible problems of alcohol abuse in clients from ethnic minorities. At present it does seem that few people from ethnic minority groups come along for help with drinking problems, either to specialist agencies or to statutory social work departments. It is important, therefore, for Social Services to liaise more effectively with ethnic-minority community groups in order to promote more information and knowledge about available services.

A study in Coventry, again of Asian communities, suggested that the Punjabi–Sikh community had a higher level of alcohol problems than others, and the Moslem community a lower level, and that there is a lack of knowledge within these communities about the effects of alcohol, and the problems it may cause (Nyak 1985). Obviously there is much work still to be done in the area of identifying the extent of problem drinking in different ethnic minorities, helping them to recognise the problem, and offering help in a way which is both accessible and acceptable, when, for instance, men and women from certain cultures may find it much more difficult to obtain and to accept help. One way forward might include employing significant numbers of specialist workers from ethnic minorities to assist in the provision of services which are particularly sensitive to culture and family tradition. Additionally, white social workers need to be aware of, and act upon, racism which permeates society's attitudes to non problem drinking ethnic minorities.

The role of the organisation

So, there is extensive and abundant evidence which would suggest that alcohol problems are an intrinsic part of the work that Social Services and Social Work Departments have to deal with. Sadly, it is also generally true that social workers do not receive firm, clear support from their departments. The BASW Policy Document states: 'Since it (alcohol), affects so many parts of the department and so many client groups, there is a need for a well-thought-out policy and strategy covering all aspects of a department's work' (BASW 1989). The SWSG Practice Guidance paper reiterates that drink problems play a part in the problems of some clients already being worked with by social work staff; that alcohol problems are often missed, and goes on to say that 'Action is required to change this situation'. They target 'senior staff who have responsibility for developing policy and planning and managing services' as one group whose participation is particularly important if 'changes in attitudes, skills and available services' are to be achieved (Social Work Services Group 1987:35).

We have already identified the need for training, and the importance of the provision of good supervision and support systems if clients with alcohol problems and their families are to be helped. This, too, is a responsibility of management. One other most important role which management must play in this process is that of ensuring good working relationships with other agencies which are also involved with those with alcohol problems – generic agencies such as hospitals, general practitioners, the police, education; and specialist agencies like Councils on Alcohol, Community Alcohol Teams, Alcohol Problem Clinics, hostels, Alcoholics Anonymous, Al-Anon, and Al-Ateen. These relationships vary from joint planning, funding, and management at senior management level to good local liaison about local resources and individual cases. The need for joint working and liaison in the field of alcohol problems, and the difficulties involved, was highlighted in a research study into the relationship among agencies coming into contact with people with alcohol problems in Lothian. This stressed the importance of good liaison among generic agencies at local level; between the generic agencies and specialist agencies, and among senior management of all agencies involved (Tavistock Institute of Human Relations 1981). This theme is repeated by Gawlinski and Otto, who state that 'how agencies and different professionals collaborate together can have a profound effect on long term treatment progress' (Gawlinski and Otto 1985:180).

Table 2.4 Barriers to good practice

Politics	Central government is confused or ambivalent about services. Speaks with forked tongue; i.e. expects much, gives too little, changes mind often
Policy	There is an absence of agreed policy about services at a national, regional, and local level
Planning	No clear plan exists for services nationally, regionally, or locally. Investment in buildings, people, and services is haphazard
Professional	Different professional groups are competing for power, mystique, status, and collectively devaluing clients' views, needs, and opinions
People	Managers — uncommitted / Planners — are — disenchanted / Researchers — personally — tired / Fieldworkers — cynical
Practice	Working methods are ill-defined. Research findings are ignored and no good theoretical basis for work exists. Training is poor or non-existent
	↓
	Intervention is likely to be misplaced, confused, inappropriate or non-existent

Source: Gawlinski and Otto 1985:184.

Gawlinski and Otto also examine the atmosphere within agencies and how this affects the delivery of services. Through working with a large number of agencies as trainers or management consultants, they were able to identify 'barriers to good practice' – see Table 2.4. This is not an optimistic view. It identifies problems throughout the systems dealing with alcohol problems, and sees them as both rational and emotional in origin. They were, however, also able to identify 'core conditions for effective service delivery' (see Table 2.5). These conditions for effective service yet again stress the need for commitment from all parts of the organisation. We will return to these components later.

Table 2.5 Core conditions for effective service delivery

Organisational	Core condition	Client/Worker
The agency has effectively researched and understood client need. It is clear about its goals and working methods.	Clarity	Good assessment. Clear agreement as to goals of intervention, time scale, and working methods.
Other people, especially consumers, understand what the agency is offering	Congruence	The intervention being used is appropriate
Recruitment, training, and staffing levels are correct	Competence	The worker is skilled, knowledgeable, and experienced
The worker is well supervised and supported with adequate working conditions	Confidence	The consumer is willing to be helped, believes she will be helped, and trusts the worker concerned. The worker is confident about her role/task
Local services are co-ordinated and planned effectively. Some element or agreement exists *vis-à-vis* working methods and core philosophy, agencies trust and respect each other's work	Continuity	Long-term support is available to those who need it. The consumer can move/ be referred between agencies without disrupting her confidence or progress

Source: Gawlinski and Otto 1985:183.

Given the complexity of the difficulties outlined, and the degree of pessimism in social work about working with those with alcohol problems, it is appropriate to examine ways in which social work can respond effectively.

Existing skills

At practitioner level, social workers already have interventive skills which are particularly helpful in working with problem drinkers, for example in interviewing and assessment, but *they may not fully appreciate this fact.* These skills include the use of systems approaches, Rogerian counselling, crisis intervention, and task-centred work.

Systems thinking is particularly useful in working with problem drinkers, as it helps to see the drinker within a series of overlapping and interrelated social systems – of agencies, communities, community groups, family, friends, workplace, etc. Hunt and Harwin point to the need for being aware of the drinker's whole situation, which includes the community he/she lives in, its attitudes to drinking, and the importance of assessing the significance of all its aspects to the client's drinking and alcohol-related problems (Hunt and Harwin 1979). It is important to locate which system(s) provide support for continuing problem-drinking behaviour, and which put the drinker under pressure to change. Social work is in a unique position to help because of the knowledge and contact which individual workers have with individual clients and their families, and the placing of teams of social workers in communities, which gives them important information about the social norms relevant to each community. Also, social workers have access to their own and other resources, which might be of help, either with the drinking problem itself, or with some of the difficulties linked with alcohol abuse, e.g. debts, unpaid gas bills, arrears with electricity payments, housing problems, marital difficulties.

It may require attention by social work to more than one system to help the drinker who decides to do something about their problem. He/she may lose support from one system such as friends who had encouraged continued drinking, while another system, for example, the workplace, may be sceptical about any change in drinking habits. However, he/she may receive support from the family system in attempts to cut down or stop. The understanding that a change in the drinker's drinking habits, even if it is for the better, will have an unsettling effect on the family system, can help the social worker help the family through a difficult period of change. For example, the parent who stops drinking will wish to take back roles and responsibilities which other family members have accepted and become accustomed to (Leckie 1979; see also Chapter 5).

Although knowledge about alcohol is an important element in helping, and there are techniques being developed which are proving particularly effective (see Chapter 3), there is evidence to suggest that the style of the worker, and the relationship the worker and client build up is also vital. If it is often the case that 'problem drinkers are involved in relationships characterised by mistrust, misunderstanding, arguments, and conflict' (Collins *et al.* 1988:18), it is important to develop a helping relationship which emphasises trust, dependability, understanding, acceptance, and encouragement. In a research study of problem drinkers who had been through an in-patient programme, they ranked these attributes as the most helpful among their therapeutic experiences (Cartwright 1986). These are skills which social workers should feel confident about possessing and using with problem drinkers. Rogerian counselling has a significant contribution to make, with its emphasis on openness, warmth, respect, and, perhaps most important of all, 'accurate empathy', i.e. listening to what the client has to say and attempting to reflect it back (Rogers 1969). Focusing on the client and encouraging him/her to explore thoughts, feelings, and conflicts is encouraged by Miller in his work on motivational interviewing (Miller 1983) and this type of counselling has been found to contribute to successful outcomes in work with problem drinkers (Miller and Baca 1983).

Social workers are no strangers to crises, as coping with crises in the lives of clients is an integral part of the social work task (O'Hagan 1986). Crisis intervention is of particular relevance to work with problem drinkers, in whose lives crises of one kind or another are not uncommon – in relation to offending, accidents, financial problems, housing, work, health, or relationships. Crises are viewed not as devastating events, but as situations where normal problem solving and coping mechanisms have failed. However, with help the client not only can be enabled to recover equilibrium, but the situation also contains the possibilities for potential growth. Crisis work is usually short-term, and in the first interview, focus, direction, and engaging the client are seen as important issues for social workers. Crisis Theory stresses that 'the client's level of hope and motivation to change will be increased if the social worker focuses on work with (rather than for) the client' (Hunt and Harwin 1979:139). Thus clients are encouraged to define for themselves the problems they wish to deal with, and examine ways of responding to them. This model also has implications for the worker, as clients are encouraged to take full part in the decision-making process, and challenge the worker to justify what he/she is suggesting, thus increasing the client's self-esteem. Hunt emphasises, however, that the client with alcohol problems should not be expected to take too much responsibility too quickly (Hunt 1982).

The Crisis Intervention model contains some of the elements of the task-centred approach, which also focuses, within specific time limits, on the client's current problems. This approach is useful with drink problems because it breaks down complex and confusing difficulties and enables the client to define specific problems and set manageable tasks and clear methods of achieving them. This process itself may give the client hope that change is not as impossible as it might have seemed. It also reinforces the client's resolve in that small changes can be seen to happen quite quickly, and the client's confidence can be enhanced for him/her to attempt more difficult changes.

Table 2.6 Frameworks for assessment

Theoretical framework	Psychosocial theory	Crisis theory	Systems approach to family therapy
Rationale	Present difficulties are the current expression of problems arising from past experience	Crisis is a precipitant of change in the client and their family	Change is dependent on a readjustment in role expectations and behaviour
Aim of assessment process	To identify the strengths and weaknesses of the client and the significant others in their social situation	To identify the area on which help should focus through analysis of the current situation	To identify roles taken by individual family members, and to check these against role ideals held
Interview situation	Usually individual client and their most significant relative seen separately	Client and significant relative may be seen separately or jointly	All the significant members of the family present together
Worker style	Eliciting information and feelings	Clarifying situation and identifying focus for help	Observing inter-action and reflecting it back to the family
Focus	Early personal history and the development of relationship patterns	Client's account of the development and meaning of current crisis	Family roles and interaction in the here-and-now situation

Source: Hunt and Harwin 1979:136.

Hunt and Harwin provide a useful table outlining the components of Crisis Theory, Psychosocial Theory, and Systemic approaches to families, which are relevant in assessing problem drinkers (see Table 2.6). It should be stressed, of course, that these are not mutually exclusive, and elements of all three might be used in the same assessment.

Tom Leckie

Transferrable skills

Apart from the interventive skills drawn from traditional social work approaches, which are particularly helpful in working with problem drinkers, there are additional knowledge and skills which can be transferred from existing social work theory. In particular, skills, associated with the 'process' model of social intervention provided on most social work courses, which consider contact in work with clients from beginning to end of the helping process. These include an examination of initial contacts, assessment, goal setting, contract making, reassessment, and termination.

Social workers will be aware of the importance of assessment and familiar with the process, providing, as it does, impressions, information, and facts, and an opportunity to review present and past difficulties with the client. Hunt gives details of an assessment interview. She stresses that 'the knowledge and skills employed are those the social worker would expect to use in the course of the initial assessment of any newly referred client' (Hunt 1982:41). The components emphasised are the collecting of information; the sensitive following up of relevant issues; reassurance; direct, but not overintrusive questioning; listening and responding to the client's questions; explaining; imparting information; sharing assessment; and negotiating of short-term work with the client.

Social workers also have to bring to the assessment process with a client who is experiencing alcohol problems, knowledge of the effect of alcohol on the individual and family, society's attitude to alcohol use and misuse, and resources available for problem drinkers in the local community (see Chapter 1).

Assessment of drinking problems requires clear details of where, when, how often, and how much drinking has been done, and with whom; and which combinations of these are most problematic. This detailed information is necessary to help the client and worker begin to identify any relationship between the client's drinking and problems being experienced. However, social workers should be careful not to allow examination of the client's personal history, the beginnings of their alcohol abuse, and the damage caused to themselves and others to dominate early interviews, as this can increase anxiety and guilt in clients, and make progress more difficult. Assessment interviews should concentrate on helping the client understand the links between alcohol use and immediate problems the client feels the need to resolve. This work is perhaps best taken forward by the use of short-term contracts, set up carefully with the client, with clear, specific goals to be achieved. Chapter 3 will focus on this area.

Social workers should also be prepared to offer advice to problem drinkers about what methods are available to help them, and what resources are on offer which might be appropriate. Some clients may need only one interview to help identify the part alcohol plays in their problems and what they wish to do about it. This area, of advice giving and contact with other resources, is a problematic one for social workers in relation to alcohol problems. Chapter 1 has already identified and examined some of the specialist alcohol resources available. These will, of course, vary from place to place. Whatever these resources are, it is one of the tasks of social workers to be aware of them. In this, they should expect the support of their agency's information systems to provide details of resources. I would suspect that the provision of this kind of useful information is uncommon. Even with it, we have already identified earlier in this chapter that social workers are liable to suffer from anxiety about role adequacy, role support, and role legitimacy in their work with problem drinkers (Shaw *et al.* 1978). This uncertainty and lack of confidence where it exists, will influence the decisions social workers make about what they do with clients with alcohol problems once they have recognised and assessed them.

The role of other agencies

The danger is that if social workers feel they lack confidence, support, and legitimacy, then they will be inclined to refer clients on to other agencies for continued support, abrogating their role in helping the client with alcohol problems. There are, of course various paths to take. Some choices are outlined below:

1. Refer to a specialist agency and ask them to deal with the drinking problem.
2. Refer to a specialist agency for 'treatment', then take up work with client at a later stage.
3. Refer to a specialist agency for assessment of drinking problems only.
4. Ask a specialist agency for advice about how to work with the client's drinking problem.
5. Ask a specialist agency for information about the client's drinking problems.
6. Ask a specialist agency for consultation about the client.
7. Make use of line management for supervision about the client.
8. Use the agency's own alcohol specialist for advice, information, consultation, supervision.

Causes for optimism

Clients with alcohol problems, and their families might need a variety of different kinds of specialist help – medical and/or psychiatric intervention for a few, AA/Al-Anon/Al-Ateen for some, referral to Councils on Alcohol or Community Alcohol Teams for others.

However, the social worker has a crucial role, identified earlier, of being aware of the needs of the client and the client's family; knowledgeable about the community the client lives in; and having access to resources which can be of help. If we add to this, knowledge about alcohol problems and confidence in using existing skills, then social workers in their intervention can be highly effective, and can do much to improve the overall quality of service to people with alcohol problems who are known to social work. Peter Abel produced 'Alcohol Abuse: Guidelines for Professionals' for Avon Social Services, and this, the recently published BASW's *Practice Guidelines*, and Social Work Services' *Practice Guidance* are evidence that social workers are not without help in this area (Abel 1983; BASW 1989; SWSG 1987).

Policy issues

Practitioners in their work with individual clients and their families can therefore play a vital part in maintaining, developing, and improving the service. This can only happen, however, in the context of a commitment from central and local agencies. Much that is positive is already being achieved. There is now no lack of advice from central departments, from the Department of Health and Social Security's 1978 report on *The Pattern and Range of Services* to the Scottish Health Education Co-ordinating Committee's report of 1985 – *Health Education in the Prevention of Alcohol-related Problems*, and more recently, BASW's *Policy Guidelines* (DHSS 1978; SHECC 1985; BASW 1989).

A growing body of research about the incidence of alcohol problems in social work, has been quoted earlier in this chapter. However, more research needs to be undertaken by local authorities and research establishments to clarify, for example, the indentification rate of alcohol problems in social work, the place of alcohol problems in generic social work, and with specific client groups like work with older people, as well as the attitudes of social work staff to alcohol problems, and the incidence of alcohol problems among social work staff.

Local authority Social Services and Social Work Departments have a crucial role to play. There are obvious difficulties to be overcome; alcohol problems do not score high marks politically, and councillors may not support initiatives. Other priorities, particularly child care may take precedence, despite evidence to suggest that alcohol problems play a significant part in child-care cases (Hebblethwaite 1982). And important initiatives planned, financed, managed, and delivered jointly with health authorities and voluntary agencies are fraught with problems. The Tavistock Institute of Human Relations (TIHR) study clearly illustrated problems in the areas of interpersonal, interprofessional and inter-organisational co-operation, and made some recommendations about how some of these difficulties might be addressed (TIHR 1981). Some statutory social work agencies, such as Newcastle, Hereford, Bradford, Strathclyde, Rotherham, Avon, Central, and Lothian have taken initiatives in the form of policy documents, research, training, support, resources, or joint-working arrangements, but more has to be done.

Unfortunately, few Social Services and Social Work Departments have specialist workers in the alcohol or addiction fields. BASW's *Policy Guidelines* identify a recent growth of specialists with specific responsibility for alcohol and/or drugs, but suggest that this role needs additional development. They stress the usefulness of a specialist at Principal Officer level, whose remit might include 'consultancy' to the department, and some resonsibility for training, developing policy, and liaising at significant levels with other agencies (BASW 1989).

Furthermore, few statutory agencies have identified the role of residential care for people with alcohol problems. The vast majority of such care is at present provided by voluntary agencies, although, for example, Lothian Region run a hostel for people with drink problems, which was developed from an innovatory local authority project in the 1970s into homelessness.

Each department should have a policy, which the BASW policy document suggests should cover issues of prevention, inter-agency co-operation, and education and training as well as direct service provision, and look at the need for specialist posts or advisors (BASW 1989). The policy should identify the resources needed to help problem drinkers in the area served by the local authority, focusing on which resources the local authority should provide, which might be provided jointly with health, and which might best be provided by voluntary agencies, perhaps grant-aided by Social Work Departments. In designing such a policy, Social Services and Social Work Departments might take into account some of the work done in the mental health field, where Community Mental Health Teams and Centres are being developed (see Chapter 1).

We should not ignore the fact, however, that more commitment often means more resources, with which most departments are not overendowed. Many of the improvements outlined previously though, do not require vast funds, as much as commitment to change the present position. What is needed to at least partly remove the 'Barriers to Good Practice', as identified by Gawlinski and Otto, and replace them with the 'Core Conditions for Effective Service Delivery', is not just significant amounts of new resources (though appropriate new resources would surely help), but, as they say, 'Clarity, Congruence, Competence, Confidence and Continuity' (Gawlinski and Otto 1985:183) – in fact, efficient planning, managing, and implementation. A similar prescription might be effective in offering some relief to the cycle of deprivation in alcohol services highlighted previously in this chapter by means of 'The Vicious Circle'. Perhaps the German scientist referred to in Leckie *et al.* makes the most apposite point. Speaking about why America was first to land on the moon, he made the point that the most important factor was not the technology nor the cost, but the will to carry it through (Leckie *et al.* 1984). As this book will amply confirm, social work does not lack the 'technology' to tackle alcohol problems at practitioner, management, or training levels, but its application and focus certainly should be sharpened.

However, in the next chapter we will move on to consider some of the most recent developments in counselling individual problem drinkers. In particular, we shall draw upon contributions from social learning theory. The chapter will emphasise the necessity for specific assessment and goal setting. It will include an examination of helping styles, the significance of relapse, the place of controlled drinking, minimal interventions, and alcohol education courses in assisting problem drinkers.

© 1990 Tom Leckie

References

Abel, P.M. (1983) *Alcohol Related Problems in Current Social Work Cases*, Avon: Social Services Department.

Behling, D.W. (1979) 'Alcohol abuse as encountered in 51 instances of reported child abuse', *Clinical Paediatrics* 18(2):57–91.

Bennett, T. and Wright, R. (1984) 'The relationship between alcohol use and burglary', *British Journal of Addiction* 79:431–43.

British Association of Social Workers (1989) *Policy Guidelines*.

British Association of Social Workers (1989) *Practice Guidelines*.

Birleson, P. and Whigmore, A. (1987) 'Suffer the little children at the hands of drink', *Social Services Insight* 12 June.

Cartwright, A. (1986) 'Is treatment an effective way of helping clients resolve difficulties associated with alcohol?' in N. Heather, I. Robertson, and P. Davies (eds) *The Misuse of Alcohol*, London: Croom Helm.

Collins, S., Ottley, G., and Wilson, M. (1988) 'Counselling problem drinkers and social work education in Scotland', *Social Work Education* 7(3):17–24.

Collins, S. and Tate, D. (1988) 'Alcohol related offenders and a voluntary organisation in a Scottish community', *The Howard Journal* 27(1), February.

Coope, G. (1979) 'The probation service and drink related offenders in prisons', unpublished manuscript.

Creighton, S.J. (1976) 'Trends in child abuse', fourth report of children placed on NSPCC Special Unit Registers.

Curran, J.H. and Chambers, G.A. (1982) *Social Enquiry Reports in Scotland*, Edinburgh: HMSO.

Department of Health and Social Security (1978) *The Pattern and Range of Services for Problem Drinkers*, London: HMSO.

Dickie, D. (1985) 'Central Offenders Unit fine alternative alcohol project', unpublished paper, Lothian Regional Social Work Department.

Fanti, G. (1985) Personal communication on Home Help study.

Fanti, G. (1985a) 'A study of field social work attitudes to problem drinkers', Hereford and Worcester Social Services Department.

Fanti, G. (1986) 'Now is the time to change the havoc caused by alcohol', *Social Work Today*, 18 August.

Fanti, G. (1987) 'Clients aren't the only ones with alcohol problems', *Community Care* 26 March, pp. vi–viii.

Gawlinski, G. and Otto, S. (1985) 'The anatomy of organisational melancholia', in N. Heather, I. Robertson and P. Davies (eds) *The Misuse of Alcohol*, London: Croom Helm.

Ghosh, S.K. (1984) 'Prevalence study of drinking alcohol and alcohol dependence in the Asian population in the UK', in N. Krasner, J.S. Madden and R. Walker (eds) *Alcohol Related Problems*.

Gloucester Probation Service (1984) Annual Report.

Goodman, C. (1981) 'A study of social workers' knowledge and attitudes to alcohol related problems in Newcastle', Alcohol Studies Centre.

Goodman, C. (1984) Unpublished research findings.

Hebblethwaite, D. (1982) 'Problem drinkers', *Community Care*, 13 May.

Hunt, L. (1982) *Alcohol Related Problems*, London: Heinemann Educational Books.

Hunt, L. and Harwin, J. (1979) 'Social work theory and practice', in M. Grant and P. Gwinner (eds) *Alcohol in Perspective*, London: Croom Helm.

Isaacs, J. and Moon, G. (1985) 'Alcohol problems – the social work response', Portsmouth: Social Services Research and Intelligence Unit.

Jeffs, B. and Saunders, W. (1983) 'Minimising alcohol related offending by enforcement of existing legislation', *British Journal of Addiction* 78:67–77.

Leckie, T. (1979) 'Intervention in alcohol problems', *Social Work Today* 10(41):13–15.

Leckie, T., Osborn, A., and Grimes, A. (1984) 'Alcoholics: too anony-mous?' *Social Work Today* 16(4):16–17.

Longman, A. (1985) Unpublished diploma dissertation.

McGarva, S. (1979) 'The measurement of alcohol abuse in social workers' caseloads', dissertation, Paisley College Alcohol Studies Centre.

Miller, W.R. (1983) 'Motivational interviewing with problem drinkers', *Behavioural Psychology* 11:147–72.

Miller, W.R. and Baca, L.M. (1983) 'Two-year follow-up of bibliotherapy and therapist-directed controlled drinking training for problem drinkers', *Behaviour Therapy* 14.

Myers, T. (1982) 'Alcohol and violent crime re-examined: self reports from two sub-groups of Scottish male prisoners', *British Journal of Addictions* 77(4).

Newcastle City Council Social Services Department Policy Division (1986) 'Children in care – a contribution to the current debate'.

Nyak, J. (1985) 'Drinking and drinking problems in Asian communities in Coventry', Coventry and Warwickshire: Alcohol Advisory Service.

O'Hagan, K. (1986) *Crisis Intervention in Social Services*, London: Macmillan.

Oliver, J.E. (1985) 'Successive generations of child maltreatment; social and medical disorders in the parents', *British Journal of Psychiatry* 147: 484–90.

Orford, J. *et al.* (1984) 'Adult children of problem drinking parents', final research report to DHSS.

Osborn, A. and Leckie, T. (1980) 'Alcohol problems and social work cases', Lothian Region Social Work Department.

Royal College of Psychiatrists (1979) *Alcohol and Alcoholism*, London: Tavistock.

Rogers, C.R. (1969) *Freedom to Learn*, Columbus: Charles E. Merrill.

Scottish Health Education Co-ordinating Committee (1985) *Health Education in the Prevention of Alcohol Problems*, Edinburgh: Scottish Health Education Group.

Scottish Home and Health Department (1981) *Statistics for 1981*, Edinburgh: HMSO.

Shaw, S. Cartwright, A., Spratley, T., and Harwin, J. (1978) *Responding to Drinking Problems*, London: Croom Helm.

Social Work Services Group (1988) *Practice Guidance – Towards Effective Practice with Problem Drinkers*, Edinburgh: Social Work Services Group, Scottish Education Department.

Strathclyde Regional Council (1981) 'A report of the Strathclyde Regional Council Social Work Standby Service', Strathclyde: Regional Council.

Tavistock Institute of Human Relations (1981) *Alcohol Related Problems: a study of inter-organisational relations*, Scottish Institute for Operational Research.

Tether, P. and Robinson, D. (1986) *Preventing Alcohol Problems. A Guide To Local Action*, London: Tavistock Publications.

Zimberg, S. (1978) 'Psychosocial treatment of elderly alcoholics', in S. Zimberg, J. Wallace, and S. Blume (eds) *Practical Approaches to Alcoholism Psychotherapy*, New York: Plenum.

Chapter three

Helping problem drinkers – some new developments

Steve Baldwin

The underlying assumption is that drinking is one example of a range of addictive behaviours, which are learned habits, developed and maintained by the principles of rewards and punishments. The growth of social learning theory, cognitive psychology, and the experimental analysis of behaviour has promoted interest in self-control and self-management perspectives, in contrast to more traditional 'disease' or 'illness' models of problem drinking. These developments have focused on an active involvement of drinkers in the resolution of their problem behaviours, with the promotion of individualised intervention programmes.

Self-management of problem drinking

Traditional disease models of alcohol have been based on the physical aspects of the drug, and its effects on individuals. In particular, these models have emphasised biological, biochemical, or physiological consequences of alcohol ingestion. These approaches have produced associated beliefs about narrow limits to self-control exerted by problem drinkers: in particular, the belief that people who have drink problems cannot control their own drinking, and are not responsible for its consequences. This 'moral code' of addictive behaviours, although still popular amongst some professional groups, has been challenged by field-work practitioners, due to its restrictive and limited utility.

Similarly, disease models of drinking have offered limited utility for field workers. The removal of personal responsibility for drinking behaviour, associated with beliefs in such medico-physical models, produced intractable problems for field workers who attempted to assist problem drinkers towards independence and problem resolution. In addition, disease models required drinkers to reduce their problems via abstinence from alcohol: whilst these models were based on 'loss of control' to explain problem drinking, they required drinkers to 'achieve control' via total abstinence. As most interventions with problem drinkers will end in a relapse, the application of disease models often has been countertherapeutic due to unrealistic expectations of clients. Self-control models of addictive behaviour, in contrast, have been based on a different set of assumptions about the nature of the development, maintenance, and resolution of human problems. Drinking behaviours (and smoking, substance abuse, overeating, and gambling behaviours) have been viewed as variants on a continuum of frequency, intensity, and duration. Such behaviours have been conceptualised as overlearned habit disorders, governed by general laws of learning theory. Whilst this model does not discount secondary physical consequences of addictive behaviours (e.g. cirrhosis, neuritis, ulcers, brain damage), it does not imply the behaviour is a disease, or that it has been caused by underlying biochemical, physiological, or neurological disorders.

This focus on social learning theory (e.g. Mahoney 1974) has shifted the emphasis to a consideration of determinants of drinking behaviour, including situational and environmental factors such as: family history, drinking peers, and personal factors such as: beliefs, attitudes, and past learning history. This has required consideration of both antecedents and consequents of the behaviour (i.e. what happens before and after drinking occurs). The application of applied behaviour analysis to problem drinking patterns has produced greater understanding of the development of maladaptive addictive patterns. It has also helped to identify the characteristics of non-problem patterns, based on moderate or controlled drinking.

This involvement of problem drinkers in self-control and self-management programmes has been based on a model of personal change based on the acquisition of new skills and strategies. Personal awareness and self-responsibility have been implicit in the model, to enable problem drinkers to move towards re-education and acquisition of new skills. In contrast to traditional disease models, the self-control model has promoted a range of outcome goals, an educational approach, skills acquisition, and cognitive or behavioural interventions (Marlatt and Parks 1982).

The development of cognitive–behavioural models of problem drinking behaviours identified specific elements required to maximise the effectiveness of interventions with clients. In particular, self-control programmes should be potent to maintain behaviour change when measured in the future at follow-up, and ensure client adherence to the programme. It should contain elements which are both behavioural (e.g. increased assertion skills by 'saying no') and cognitive (e.g. distraction 'by thinking of something else') and should enhance personal motivation to promote the maintenance of behaviour change. Similarly, it should substitute maladaptive patterns with alternative behaviours which achieve gratification and seek to promote generalised coping skills in new situations. Last, the programmes should aim to teach new methods of coping with 'failure' experiences (relapse prevention), increase self-efficacy in problem situations, and use the client's support systems to enhance the generalisation of coping skills (Marlatt and Gordon 1985).

Intervention with drinkers: relapse prevention

Self-control models of problem drinking have included explicit consideration of the situations in which clients violate previous decisions to reduce or abstain from drinking. Such relapses relate to the breaking of self-imposed rules which govern the rate or pattern of drinking behaviour (Marlatt and Gordon 1980). These may include an initial lapse (the first 'rule violation') and subsequent relapse (when the first drink has been followed by a binge, or uncontrolled drinking).

The 'Relapse Prevention' model has been based on an assumption about the achievement of perceived control by the drinker to maintain his or her drinking rules. Such control will continue until the drinker encounters a high-risk situation, which imposes a threat to self-control, or increases the probability of relapse. Whilst various high-risk situations have been identified, three specific situations have recurred in analyses of relapse episodes. These include:

(1) Negative emotional states (e.g. 'I felt so low after getting fired, I just had to have a drink');
(2) Interpersonal conflicts (e.g. 'My partner wouldn't believe I hadn't been out drinking, so I thought I might just as well anyway'); and
(3) Social pressure (e.g. 'All my mates were drinking and giving me a hard time about staying on orange juice, so I went ahead, back on the drink').

According to the Relapse Prevention model, decreased probabilities of relapse will occur if the individual is able to complete a planned coping strategy in the high-risk situation. Also, if successful, the individual will be more likely to expect to cope successfully with high-risk situations in the future. Increased probabilities of relapse occur if the individual holds positive expectations about the immediate positive effects of alcohol, at the expense of consideration of the delayed negative consequences (e.g. 'A drink would help me through this difficult court appearance'). Inability to cope in high-risk situations, coupled with positive beliefs about coping through old habitual behaviours, will maximise the probability of an initial lapse. When individuals who were committed to abstinence drink alcohol, characteristic reactions of dissonance (conflict and guilt) and personal attribution (self-blaming) may occur. This 'Abstinence Violation Effect' (AVE) (Marlatt and Gordon 1980) has been recorded in many self-reports from problem drinkers, and may account for self-statements such as: 'This just goes to show I can't control my drinking once it starts' and 'I have no willpower, I may as well go ahead'.

Relapse Prevention has produced a shift of intervention style with problem drinkers. Whilst traditional approaches have used confrontive techniques to overcome denial, the RP strategy has focused on drinking behaviours, not on the so-called 'personality' of the drinker. Also, it has required clients with drink problems to maintain an active participation in their own programme, in contrast to the 'passive victim' approach characteristic of disease models. RP goals include: the development of increased awareness and choice of behaviour; increased coping skills; and greater self-control. These goals may be achievable through recognition of and coping with high-risk situations (such as being out with other people who are drinking), and modification of behaviour patterns to prevent a lapse from developing into 'full-blown' relapse.

In particular, the identification of high-risk situations will require the use of self-monitoring techniques such as behavioural assessment. This might include self-recording methods such as drink diaries. Similarly, relapse fantasies are produced, using imagined descriptions of future lapses. This technique requires the client to 'think through' future situations where a relapse is most likely to occur. The absence of adequate coping responses would be resolved by relaxation training to improve coping skills in difficult situations. Self-management techniques or specific skills training (e.g. via relapse rehearsal) also might be included. Improved performance may require information and education about immediate and delayed consequences of alcohol ingestion. Subsequent use of alcohol will require an agreed contract to limit the extent of drinking and 'reminder cards' to assist coping if a slip occurs. Reminder cards are used to give specific instructions to clients who lapse in difficult situations, and are carried by clients at all times. Such instructions might read: 'You have had one or two drinks.

You can still stop, however. It is not necessary for you to continue drinking. If you leave now, you can stop.' Such a programme may also involve a 'programmed relapse' (where initial use occurs under supervised conditions).

The application of RP programmes with problem drinkers can be of benefit to social work practitioners. This application, however, requires some knowledge of learning theory, cognitive–behavioural therapy, self-control theory, and drinking behaviour. As most social work training courses do not include such material, individual practitioners will need to acquire such information and skills from reading relevant literature and by attending specific post-qualification courses. Skilled application of RP programmes will require supervision from an experienced practitioner (for example, from a clinical psychologist or an alcohol counsellor) and/or advanced training in the application of self-control procedures. In particular, screening skills are required to identify situations where RP programmes are contraindicated. For example, RP is inappropriate when there is clear evidence of physical damage due to prolonged alcohol abuse. Individuals with psychotic behaviours also will be unlikely to benefit from this approach.

Skilled helping with problem drinkers

Social work practitioners often do not feel competent or adequate in their work with problem drinkers (see Chapter 2). Whilst this may reflect some common negative stereotypes about problem drinkers shared by other professional groups such as GPs and nurses (Clement 1986), it is more plausibly explained by defects in social work education, post-qualification experiences, and inadequate in-service training opportunities.

The acquisition of basic counselling or helping skills is a prerequisite for work with problem drinkers and should be part of the repertoire of all social workers. Whilst Relapse Prevention or motivational interview techniques should be within the competency limits of many social work practitioners, these procedures also require some basic and intermediate skills. At least, practitioners should achieve competence at choosing from a flexible range of intervention styles with drinkers. Practitioners who have remained inept have contributed to a negative climate towards counselling and psychotherapy (Strupp *et al.* 1977). Furthermore, client deterioration should be avoided (Bergin 1980).

Fundamental intervention skills required for field-work practitioners should include: basic and advanced communication skills; skills to help clients challenge themselves; problem clarification;

skills in goal setting; and the development, implementation, and evaluation of the client's own programme (Egan 1986). Competence in these areas will be related to an appreciation of social work theory and practice skills, applied developmental psychology, knowledge about alcohol, the social settings of clients, and the power of culture.

Establishment of an active, co-operative approach when working with problem-drinking clients requires achievement of a goal of self-responsibility. Whilst client self-responsibility may be undermined by specific patterns such as passivity in the face of problems, learned helplessness, and disabling self-talk, it may be promoted by enhancement of personal coping skills. The establishment of an effective helping relationship also requires an appreciation of factors likely to enhance the helping process: attractiveness (the perceived similarity of the social worker to the client); trustworthiness of the worker (honesty, lack of personal gain, openness); social worker competence (ability, skill to help). 'Competence' is clearly more than role-competence. Whilst many social workers view themselves as qualified professionals, they may lack competence in reputation with some clients and in their own skills repertoire. Hence, the move into effective work with problem drinkers should be based on generic knowledge and skills, and some more specialised skills (see Chapter 2).

The fundamental axis for all counselling work remains the therapeutic contract. As implicit and explicit contracts govern virtually all interactions between workers and clients, social workers should acquire skills in formulating and negotiating contracts with drinking clients. Both practitioner and drinker should 'own' the agreed goals and procedures of the helping intervention. The contract can help to provide the structure for the programme through a clarification of methods (Corden and Preston-Shoot 1988; Shapiro 1968; Wollersheim *et al.* 1980).

Clients with drink problems frequently do not recognise the nature of the dimensions of their drinking (or even of the existence of a problem). Such clients may be referred to social work practitioners as involuntary referrals, or following contact from a third party (for example, via a spouse or another family member). This initial work with problem drinkers often involves exploration of the problem, by identification of its parameters, and clarification of its consequences and implications.

'Ownership' of the helping process by problem drinkers can be assisted through use of techniques such as contracting, and active collaboration with the person to achieve problem identification. Problem drinkers who have been referred by other persons may find it difficult to focus on their own problems, and instead focus on the failings of others. These clients may require assistance to focus on their own situation, by redirecting them to their present circumstances. In the initial stages of working with problem drinkers, the main aim is to enable the person to present a detailed account of their drinking history, which may have evolved over several years. As many clients will have developed multiple problems related to their drinking, focusing on the *central* problem not related to drink (e.g. job loss, break up of a relationship, police arrest) will be a *prerequisite* for subsequent interventions. Many drinking clients also will need to be challenged on specific themes or topics, to overcome 'blind spots' such as the long-term physical effects of alcohol.

The achievement of clear problem identification will allow social worker and client to move towards goal setting. In general, this process will require clients to negotiate a set of steps to allow them to move towards reduced drinking, controlled drinking, or abstinence. Goals and subgoals, to be achievable, should be: clear, specific, realistic, related to the problem situation, consistent with the client's values, and manageable in days or weeks, rather than months (Egan 1986). Goal setting may be assisted by framing statements such as: '*Who* will do *what*, with *whom*, by *when*, and to *what degree of success?*'

Goal specificity is a prerequisite to successful reform attempts by problem drinkers. The selection of choices between goals may be enhanced by an examination of the consequences of several options. A formal method to examine these choices has been refined specifically for people with problems of substance abuse, and may be useful to assist clients to make decisions (see Marlatt 1979). Whilst practitioners cannot (and should not) be responsible for the choices of problem drinkers, a responsibility exists to assist clients to make informed decisions. An informed decision always requires consideration of several options: drinking clients who restrict themselves to one or two either−or options should be encouraged to see this situation as a restrictive, forced choice not an informed decision.

Skilled helping with problem drinkers will require a shift from informed decision-making (contemplation) to action. Many drinkers will be unfamiliar with realistic goal setting and many formulate unrealistic ('I must stop drinking completely – now!') or vague ('I really should do something') goals. Much assistance may be required for clear goal setting, based on achievable, smaller, initial goals. Similarly, problem drinkers may restrict their progress because of the identification of only one strategy to achieve their goal. Several strategies should be identified, any of which may achieve the desired goal.

The choice of goals and means should be part of the collaborative process between the social worker and his or her clients. Such choices should reflect the clients' own preferences, and be individualised to maximise the probability of successful achievement. Strategies should be congruent with the client's own values, and be realistic. Skilled social workers should explore ways in which the client's strategies may 'fail' to anticipate problems and plan for unexpected outcomes. Clients should understand that this process does not undermine or devalue their reform attempts, but rather has been designed to prevent subsequent relapse. This reflects the need for realism, as well as optimism, when working with problem drinkers.

Working with problem drinkers requires maximum flexibility from the social worker. Whilst specific ingredients, such as goal setting and self-management may be essential prerequisites to the resolution of problem drinking, much flexibility is required in the interpretation of these ingredients. A rigid, mechanical, 'cookbook' application of ingredients will be inappropriate to most problem drinkers, and may be rejected outright by others. For example, by necessity, social workers often start work with problem drinkers in the absence of complete information about the person and their problems. Consequently, the provision of additional information about the person will require revision of previous goals or subgoals.

Whilst working with problem drinkers requires some specialist knowledge and acquisition of specialist skills, this should be complementary to the prior assimilation of core transferable skills, such as personal warmth, genuineness, and respect. These core skills should be expressed behaviourally, in actions such as: maintenance of confidentiality, provision of an individualised and non-judgemental approach, respect for self-determination, self-assertion, openness, and a refusal to overemphasise role (Egan 1986). Such skills, expressed behaviourally, are prerequisites for working with clients with drink problems. Social workers should be familiar with these prerequisites from their training and experiences with other clients.

Intervention styles – working flexibly with problem drinkers

Social workers should also acquire a flexible range of intervention styles in working with problem drinkers. Intervention styles have been categorised into six types, within two main categories, assumed to cover all desirable and worthwhile interactions (Heron 1975). The two categories are authoritative and enabling. In the authoritative category, the counsellor adopts a more dominant or assertive position. Also, the emphasis is more on the actions of the counsellor, than those of the client. The other main category is enabling, where the counsellor is less obtrusive and more discreet; also, the emphasis is more on the effects on the client. Authoritative styles include prescriptive, informative, and confrontive interventions; enabling styles include cathartic, catalytic, and supportive interventions.

To illustrate these intervention styles, practical examples have been provided. These examples have been taken from a training video for people working with problem drinkers (Baldwin 1987).

Authoritative interventions

Prescriptive

Prescriptive interventions seek to directly influence the behaviour of the problem drinker. This style concentrates on advice, expression of a judgement, or an evaluation about the client.

Examples

(a) I advise you to reduce your drinking to 10 pints per week.
(b) Your weekly drinking has been at its highest since the beginning of the year: a reduction is necessary.

Informative

Informative interventions give instructions or new information to the client. The worker seeks to interpret the behaviour of the client by giving feedback.

Examples

(a) One more drink-related offence will increase your chances of being sent down by 25 per cent.
(b) One more drink-related offence will put you in danger of breaching your probation order.

Confrontive

These interventions confront the client with challenging or direct feedback. They provide a direct challenge to the restrictive attitudes, beliefs, or behaviours of the client.

Examples

(a) You believe your drinking is not harmful. It is. You have lost your job, your spouse, and your friends. Your high levels of drinking have produced much damage to yourself and others.

(b) You blame other people and outside events for your problems. You feel the police picked on you when you lost your licence. Also, you think your partner was unfair to leave you. It is difficult for you to accept responsibility for these events because you prefer to feel like a victim of circumstances.

Enabling interventions

Cathartic

The worker helps the client to release their tensions, by encouraging laughter, crying, feelings of fear, anger, depression, and other emotions. The true cathartic release will allow the client to experience painful or difficult feelings.

Examples

(a) Your partner's drinking has caused you much distress, but you have never let it out. They made you keep quiet about your feelings and you bottled them up. You feel angry towards them for doing that to you, that you were never allowed to tell them how you felt about their drinking. If they were here, now, what would you say to them?

(b) You have talked about feeling very guilty about your drinking. Keeping it a secret all these months has made it difficult to talk. You have misled other people about your drinking and have been deceitful to yourself. You have described how you hurt other people and caused them distress. How does that leave you feeling about yourself?

Catalytic

Catalytic interventions require the worker to be a catalyst, as in chemistry, by adding something original to existing ingredients to help a new natural reaction to occur. The worker seeks to help the client to develop and learn by self-direction and self-discovery.

Examples

(a) You have talked about feeling out of control with your drinking. You sound worried about how alcohol seems to be taking over your life. Sometimes it feels as if you would like me to make decisions for you, but I wonder if you are ready to do this yourself. Can you think of some way you can regain control of your drinking?

(b) You have talked about making changes in your lifestyle. For example, you mentioned reducing your drinking, and staying out of trouble with the boss at work. You have realised how your lunchtime drinking sessions put you at risk for the afternoon. You were asking me to help you out by phoning your employer, but I don't think I should direct your life. How might you change your drinking patterns to cut down the risks for your job?

Supportive

Supportive interventions seek to support the client by expressing approval of their value. The worker seeks to confirm the worth of the client by confirming and validating their attempts and efforts to change.

Examples

(a) I share your concern about your drinking. I understand how difficult it can be to acknowledge how alcohol has been affecting your relationship with your partner. Coming here today to start talking about your drinking is the first step in getting some help. Your appointment today is a sign that you have recognised the problem and want to do something about it.

(b) I appreciate your dilemma. You feel that if you give up drinking completely you will lose all your friends. You are facing a difficult choice and I see how distressing that would be. It is important to find a solution which you feel is acceptable, and I would like to help if I can. I can understand how this feels like a forced choice, and I agree it seems difficult, but maybe we can work something out, manageable for you.

All six types have an equal status; no particular category is more or less significant or important than another. Each type can have a high value for the client. Although most workers find it easier to become skilled with authoritative interactions, skilled social workers should be able to select from each style as required. Truly skilled work with problem drinkers requires workers to move smoothly across different intervention types. In addition to elegant transitions between styles, the skilled worker should know at all times which style they are using, and for what purpose.

Setting the conditions of change for problem drinkers

All practitioners have attempted to work with clients who did not wish to change. Many social workers will have invested hours of counselling with problem drinkers who had no intention of modifying their drinking patterns. Since 1980, a model has been developed

in the field of addictive behaviours which has produced fundamental changes in the work of many practitioners.

An analysis of eighteen leading therapeutic approaches has
examined the specific features included in each of them. These
included: preconditions for intervention, processes of change,
content to be changed, and the therapeutic relationship. In
addition, clients should bring positive expectations to the therapeutic intervention, at least to start the process of change. Similarly, client 'motivation' has been viewed as fundamental to
successful change attempts. Such motivation to change will relate
to a host of variables, such as the history of the person, their
knowledge about other options, and the availability of alternative
responses and personal choices.

Analytic work completed in clinics with smokers produced a
similar change model (Diclemente and Prochaska 1982). Smokers
who described their reform attempts to quit referred to a series of
stages during the change process:

(i) thinking about stopping smoking;
(ii) becoming determined to stop;
(iii) active modification of habits and environment;
(iv) maintaining non-smoking behaviour.

The model has favoured a cyclical, rather than linear sequence. The
'revolving door' scheme of smoking reform attempts has been confirmed both by clinic smokers, and also by clients who have quit
smoking via self-help methods. Specifically, most people who
attempt to quit smoking do not achieve this goal at the first
attempt, and return on the contemplation/determination/active
change/maintenance cycle several times. Successful non-smokers
report the need to rehearse active strategies during reform attempts
to maintain progress and avoid relapse.

This breakthrough research with smokers has been applied to
client populations with other problems such as alcohol and obesity.
It has helped to integrate the verbal and behavioural components of
change, through both an analysis of theoretical accounts of change,
and an analysis of reports of clients. One conclusion from the
model has been that both sets of processes – both verbal and
behavioural are important (Diclemente and Prochaska 1982;
Prochaska and Diclemente 1982). Thus, whilst verbal processes
help prepare clients for action, behavioural processes are more
important once clients have committed themselves to act.

Other consequences of this early work with smokers produced
novel insights into the method of change between stages (e.g. from
precontemplation to contemplation). Some shifts were due to

developmental processes related to life stages, for example, connected to reactions to age milestones; others were due to precipitating life events such as those related to divorce, marriage, and births. In addition, research into smoking behaviours found that some smokers achieved equal positive change from self-help attempts when compared with help from qualified therapists. Such findings have helped to 'revalue' clients with a more positive image, accompanied by a shift away from blaming so-called 'unmotivated' clients. In addition, the commonalities, the similarities, between successful self-help attempts and formal therapeutic interventions have produced support for this model.

Four components of change

More recently, the original model has been revised, (McConnaughy *et al.* 1984) to include four components of change: precontemplation, contemplation, action, and maintenance (Prochaska and Diclemente 1983). None the less, some clients do not progress around the stages of change, and may become 'stuck' at particular places. Many problem drinkers, whilst aware of their problems, remain in contemplation for several years, before taking action. Others never move from contemplation, and may never take action.

Successful work with problem drinkers requires that both social workers and clients focus on the same stage of change. Much resistance will occur from a discrepant focus: a contemplating client may be threatened by attempts from a practitioner who is in an 'action' stage. Both social workers and clients are at risk from being 'stuck' in a favoured stage of change.

Processes of change

The model also has predicted that clients in particular stages of change will be amenable to different processes of change. Clients who are 'contemplators' will be most open to consciousness-raising interventions, such as observations, confrontations, and interpretations by the worker. They will make good use of bibliotherapy – the provision of basic information leaflets, books – and other educational interventions. Self-re-evaluation also will occur as clients become more aware of themselves and their problems.

During the action stage, clients should be aware of their own personal reform and perceive *themselves* as the source of change. They should see their reform attempts as their own responsibility, and not attribute their successes or failures to the practitioner.

Clients who are in the action stage often are vulnerable and at risk, which may explain the importance of the 'helping relationship' and 'personal support' at this time. The knowledge that the social worker will continue to provide assistance and support may allow clients to continue their reform attempts despite problems and risks, and despite increasing probabilities of relapse.

The preparation for maintenance of positive changes will require an accurate assessment of the conditions in which relapse is most likely to occur. Whilst many drinking clients initially, may perceive this as an invitation to drink, or as an expression of doubt about their abilities, this preparation is a prerequisite to successful reforms. A sense of personal coping (Bandura 1977) will enhance the ability of clients to be assertive in dealing with difficult or threatening situations. This expression of coping will tend to increase through the stages of precontemplation, contemplation, action, and maintenance. For further details of these processes applied to groups, see Chapter 6.

Research completed with clients with a range of addictive behaviours (e.g. problem drinkers, smokers, eaters) has produced a profile of fourteen patterns of change. The four most common profiles identified in a two-year study of self-change approaches to smoking were:

(1) linear, where individuals progress from stage to stage;
(2) cyclical, where individuals take action and relapse, followed by further contemplation and more action;
(3) an unsuccessful cyclical profile;
(4) nonprogressing cyclical profile without improvement.

Practitioners working with problem drinkers may well recognise these profiles from their own work.

Levels of intervention

The model also has identified a range of levels at which interventions with clients may occur. These include:

(1) symptom/situational, for example, to reduce physical damage from drinking;
(2) maladaptive cognitions; for example, 'I am a hopeless addict';
(3) current intrapersonal conflicts;
(4) family conflicts;
(5) interpersonal conflicts.

Initial change attempts may be best directed at the symptom/situational level, because change will occur more quickly, and because it is often the prime reason for a client to start change attempts. Subsequent shifts into exploration of maladaptive cognitions, such as 'I can never stop drinking: I am out of control', and intrapersonal, family, or interpersonal conflicts will require more complex interventions and more time to achieve these goals. The model will require the social worker to intervene at any of the five levels.

This model has advanced the understanding of both researchers and practitioners in an appreciation of the conditions of change for people with addictive problem behaviours. In particular, the model has identified some of the answers to questions of what, where, when, and with whom, change may or may not occur (Prochaska and Diclemente 1986).

Motivational interviewing with clients who drink

Traditional disease models of drinking have emphasised the 'motivation' of the drinking client; people who did not change or refused to start to change were believed to be 'lacking in motivation', or 'resistant to treatment'. In addition, successful outcomes often have been ascribed not to the individual, but to the programme of intervention. This attributional bias, in favour of the practitioner, has been at the expense of the client.

The characteristic of 'denial' also has been at the core of mythologies about people with drink problems. It has been used as an explanation, as an obstacle to treatment, and as a major reason for intervention failures. Similarly, the image of drinkers as hopeless, pathological liars has been central to traditional belief systems; problem drinkers have been discredited as reliable sources of self-report about their own drinking.

In reality, however, there has been scant evidence for these pervasive stereotypes. Some of the beliefs about 'denial' may relate to common statements from drinkers such as: 'I am not an alcoholic' and 'I do not have to abstain from alcohol for the rest of my life'. Whilst these statements are entirely consistent with controlled drinking or reduced drinking goals based on a social learning perspective, they are diametrically opposed to traditional disease models, which propose abstinence as the single goal for problem drinkers. Thus, many of the stereotypes about problem drinkers may have resulted from an overapplication of inappropriate models.

A recent analysis of this phenomenon has suggested that qualities of 'resistance' and 'denial' have occurred as a function of particular practitioner styles (Miller 1983). In particular, the motivational model predicts that drinking clients will defend a polarised viewpoint, i.e. 'continue to drink' as a direct contradiction to the practitioner viewpoint of 'stop drinking completely'. This model is based on the premiss that drinking clients will adopt and defend an opposite view as a natural function of an intervention based on polarised dimensions. It also maintains that direct argument is the least efficient way to produce a change of opinion (Miller 1983).

The motivational interviewing model has emphasised consideration of both positive and negative aspects of drinking, with an exploration of these contrasting demands with the problem drinker. The accomplishment of the balance in favour of positive reform is related to several specific techniques for social workers. These include:

(1) a de-emphasis on labelling;
(2) emphasising the individual responsibility of the drinker;
(3) internal attribution;
(4) the role of cognitive dissonance.

The de-emphasis on labelling is based on a recognition that labelling of problem drinkers may be counterproductive, as well as unnecessary to positive change. The responsibility for change is placed with the client, and not with the worker; the decision to change (or not change) is left to the drinker to resolve. An internal attribution of responsibility for change will require the problem drinker to accept this for themselves, rather than externalise their successes or failures to a disease, or to the social worker. The creation of cognitive dissonance (for example, to increase the awareness of discrepancy between the beliefs and actions of a client) is viewed as an opportunity for the client to move into adaptive behaviour change, by recognition of the discrepancies between previous beliefs and 'new' realities. The emphasis is for social workers to place weighting on the positive side of the 'scales' for change.

Therefore, the direction of client motivation towards positive behaviour change will require achievement of strategic goals, including increased self-esteem, increased coping skills, and increased dissonance.

Successful motivational interviewing requires several strategies. The practitioner should increase the client's self-esteem by accurate empathy, by selective and active reflections to the client of their feelings about their own situation. The drinking client will become more aware of their own problems by their own self-motivational statements: the goal for social workers is to assist drinkers to 'talk themselves into change'. The probability of such statements from clients can be increased through use of questions such as: 'What things have you noticed about your drinking that concern you, or might be a problem?' or 'What makes you think you should do something about your drinking?' More advanced techniques include the use of paradox to enhance motivation and should be used with caution. 'Frankly I am not sure if you have enough motivation to complete this programme: maybe you don't even think you have a problem.' The use of objective assessment, for instance, data about amounts of alcohol consumption and liver test results also may be used to increase motivation for change. An accurate summary of the motivational change process should emphasise the client's positive self-change statements.

Three phases in motivational interviewing

The motivational interviewing model has been refined to include an outline of sequence for maximum effectiveness. This sequence should start with encouragement for the client to make statements, such as: 'It is in my best interests to change, I do have a problem after all', subtle, selective shaping of positive statements towards change. This process is enhanced by the provision of objective information such as a 'check-up' on the client's drinking. Specific information may be required by the drinker, which should then be provided as education to promote the decision to change.

The three phases – of self-motivation, objective information, and specific information – should then be summarised by the worker, who may present the alternatives to clients who remained undecided. If necessary, clients may be given information about the stages of change (i.e. precontemplation, contemplation, action, maintenance) to assist their understanding of their own position.

The Drinker Check-Up

More recently the motivational interviewing model has been updated and elaborated (Miller *et al*. 1988). The provision of the 'Drinker Check-Up' (DCU) has been used as a potential intervention. The Drinker Check-Up has been derived from a health-promotion model and has been used to offer individual drinkers a means for discovering the negative effects of drink on their life. A battery of measures sensitive to the effects of alcohol on health has been included in the model, together with objective feedback about personal health and levels of current functioning. It has been made available as a check-up for drinkers who would like to find out whether their drinking is doing them any harm.

The DCU has been used in conjunction with a subsequent,

follow-up, feedback session to present objective information to clients about their drinking. Potential applications also include selection of appropriate interventions, matching them to the needs of the client, and self-assessment. Test results are presented to clients as personal scores and the general tone of the DCU investigations has been: 'Let's find out about your health and drinking', rather than confrontational or diagnostic. Feedback of results has been used by practitioners to agree subsequent goals with drinking clients about reform attempts. Ideally, discussions with clients should discuss a range of options and alternatives to drinking, with a joint approach to decision-making.

The preliminary results from motivational interviewing research, and work completed on the DCU, suggest that such methods may become the first line of help in health and social service settings. Such brief interventions may be able to impact on heavy drinking and its related problems, despite the brevity of such 'minimal interventions'. The challenge for social workers who may work with high percentages of problem drinkers in their caseloads, would be to begin to incorporate such methods into their own routine practice.

Types of intervention

Controlled drinking

The choice of intervention goals with people who have drink problems has been the subject of much debate. Historically, there has been much pressure to direct clients towards abstinence goals, within a treatment ethos supported by a strong moral background. Until the 1960s, details about intervention goals other than abstinence were uncommon, or remained unreported. Publication of the seminal study of heavy drinkers who had achieved controlled drinking demonstrated that non-abstinent goals might be appropriate for some client populations (Davies 1962). Many other studies have since demonstrated that clients can achieve controlled drinking goals (Heather and Robertson 1983a). These observations have been based on rigorous and systematic research observations of controlled drinking groups.

Inconsistent usage of terms such as 'controlled drinking' has limited the use of comparisons between studies. Definitions of a 'controlled drinker' have been neither uniform nor precise. A review of the usage of non-abstinent intervention programmes (Pattison 1976), suggested that terms such as 'social drinking' be discarded in favour of the operationally more accurate 'attenuated drinking'. Other work has suggested that controlled/attenuated drinking goals may be the 'treatment of choice' with specific client groups. Moreover, abstinence goals may produce specific problems for some clients, including: impossible rehabilitation targets, a failure to join or complete intervention endeavours, the punishment of non-abstinent clients, and a failure to appreciate other goals achieved by drinkers (Pattison 1976). Several studies have stated the need for a differential assessment process, leading to individualised intervention programmes, with individualised goals.

More recent research has confirmed the validity of establishing behaviour-change programmes for problem drinkers in non-institutional settings. Many of these studies have demonstrated the benefits of non-abstinent drinking goals for groups of clients in local neighbourhood settings (e.g. Vogler *et al.* 1976). Recognition of problem drinking as: 'a reversible behavioural disorder rather than an irreversible disease' (Heather and Robertson 1983b) has shifted the focus of attention to the establishment of controlled drinking goals in intervention programmes. This has been of particular salience to people working with younger client populations who are in their teens and early twenties, who have not yet developed serious alcohol problems. Thus, whilst abstinence goals have continued to be viewed as the optimum strategy for people with chronic drink problems, controlled drinking goals often have been viewed as the 'treatment of choice' with younger, male drinkers.

The most appropriate application of controlled drinking methods may relate to interventions with early-stage problem drinkers, who would otherwise be deterred from seeking assistance by the prospect of abstinence goals. A common finding in this area has been that intensive treatments have been no more effective than various forms of 'minimal interventions' (Miller and Taylor 1980). Similarly, other studies have reported no overall differences between intensive and minimal interventions, despite some evidence for greater improvements with extensive interventions amongst clients with more severe problems. In contrast, more recent studies have reported the greater effectiveness of intensive, controlled drinking treatments compared to minimal interventions, which are based only on assessment and advice. The effective component of 'minimal interventions' may be the self-help manuals, based on behavioural principles. More recent research has suggested that the sequencing of materials related to information-giving and the teaching of skills may have an impact on outcome. In particular, there is some evidence that behavioural components should be presented first to maximise effectiveness.

Minimal interventions

An intervention may be considered 'minimal' if it entails less professional time or resources than typically involved in group, or individual, face-to-face interventions (Heather 1986). Minimal interventions may include the use of self-help manuals, with or without worker involvement. One reason for increased professional interest in minimal interventions, including the use of self-help manuals or 'bibliotherapy', has been the recognition that interventions with problem drinking may be selected from a continuum of intensity or potency.

Specifically, the distinction between 'education' and 'treatment' has become blurred, with greater focus on matching clients to interventions. Other minimal interventions have included: audio tapes, video tapes, postal contact, and telephone reporting. Another major factor has been the need to develop more cost-effective interventions for larger client populations that require service provision, despite diminishing resources.

Other advantages of minimal interventions include the reduced probability of iatrogenic effects of medicalised treatments by the use of less disease-focused materials. Also there will be a reduced probability of secondary handicapping or stigmatisation from unnecessary labelling. In addition, self-help approaches such as manuals have been developed within the framework of the scientifically based principles of self-management theory. This behavioural technology has provided the empirical framework for the development of self-help materials.

The demise of disease theories of alcohol has increased the recognition that early-stage problem drinkers provide a legitimate target for intervention attempts (Heather 1986; Heather and Robertson 1983b). In particular, this paradigm shift has prompted an increased interest in service provision based on secondary prevention to non-chronic client populations who have already developed minor alcohol problems. The use of minimal interventions also has been consistent with the recognition that abstinence goals may be counterproductive with early-stage problem drinkers.

Given the wide range of clients, problems, and interventions, the need to establish a rational basis for assignment of clients to specific interventions has remained paramount. This has been particularly salient in interventions with offenders, where few treatment-matching attempts have been established. None the less, most interventions with offenders (McGuire and Priestley 1985) have been applied in the absence of a direct focus on intervention contents, group selection, or client-specific materials (Blackburn

1980). As stated earlier, one theoretical model has proposed that the intensity of an intervention required will be determined by the stage of change reached by the client (Prochaska and Diclemente 1982). The challenge for practitioners, therefore, has been to match interventions with the state of change in clients, to maximise:

(1) the cost-effectiveness of services;
(2) the probability of success; and
(3) the probability of maintenance of therapeutic gains.

The application of minimal interventions to young offenders in small groups has been one low-cost attempt to promote therapeutic gains with an at-risk client population (McMurran 1988).

Alcohol Education Courses (AECs)

Since 1979, the development of Alcohol Education Courses has continued without systematic attempts at co-ordination, monitoring, or evaluation. In England and Wales, most AECs have been developed in Probation Services and Social Services Departments, often initiated by individual practitioners with a 'special interest' in alcohol and offending. In Scotland, until 1985, there were no attempts at systematic evaluation of the effectiveness of AECs, despite some investments from several Social Work Departments. The overall situation in the UK until 1985 was of extensive, haphazard, service provision, but without planning or evaluation. Examination of services in the UK has suggested two main origins of AECs – located at Corby in England and Dundee in Scotland.

The development of AECs has not been well documented, although some in-house publications were completed by several Social Services, Social Work, and Probation Departments. The first published account of the development of AECs was a study of the Corby Alcohol Therapy Group (Northamptonshire Probation Service 1982). The report was a service-based descriptive account of the Alcohol Therapy Group (ATG) from 1979 to 1981. As the name suggests, the ATG was provided as a 'rehabilitative' option for clients with drink-related offending. This report offered an account of the contents of the ATG programme, with supplementary demographic material about offenders who had attended. An initial before–after evaluation was planned; reconviction rates were compared for 40 cases for 12 months preceding and following the programme. A reduction from 1.77 to 1.08 offences per offender, per year, was reported.

The second report on the development of Alcohol Education Courses was based on similar work completed in Coventry (Bailey and Purser 1982). The work extended the original Corby Model to develop a court-based Alcohol Education Group (AEG) service. This was a Probation Service initiative, which subsequently was incorporated into the local Council on Alcohol. Similar to Corby, the initiative started with several 'key people', who developed the concept of alcohol education, according to a personal philosophy. Both projects were characterised by: low funding, minimal staffing, zero resources, minimal planning, and zero evaluation.

The first attempt at evaluation was based on the Alcohol Study Group in Berkshire (Singer 1983). The Alcohol Study Group was similar to the Coventry Model, with six weekly sessions of alcohol education/information designed to 'educate participants about the damage alcohol can cause' (Singer 1983). The service was court-based and operated by the Probation Service.

A before–after evaluation attempt was based on measurement of offending rates. At the 12-month follow-up, 11 offenders from a pool of 33 had re-offended (33.3 per cent); those offenders completing the course had a reconviction rate of 24.8 per cent, and those who dropped out had a reconviction rate of 62.5 per cent. Other improvements were noted, including increased knowledge of alcohol, measured by statements about the appropriateness of drinking situations, more adaptive attitudes to drinking, and reduced intake of alcohol at follow-up.

The Berkshire Project has remained the best-documented account of alcohol education work with offenders in England, Wales, and Northern Ireland. Despite its evaluation attempt, however, the generalisability of the results of this study have been restricted by design limitations. Specifically, the study was based on a weak 'before and after' design, and did not include a control group. Thus, whilst the Berkshire Report provided a useful account of process variables in alcohol education initiatives with offenders, for instance, demographic information, drop-out rates, and effectiveness data, the potency of the project was severely limited by key methodological flaws.

More recently, the Berkshire Model has been duplicated in Somerset, with some amendments to the original course contents (Menary 1986). The Somerset Alcohol Education Course has reworked many ingredients of previous alcohol education initiatives. It has, however, also included more behavioural components, including one skills-teaching session. The Somerset Model has been developed around a structure of alcohol information and behavioural self-monitoring. Whilst the initial report has not included data on effectiveness, an evaluation project has been planned.

Another study has reported preliminary findings from the first four Alcohol Education Programmes completed during 1984/85 in Devon (Godfrey and Leahy 1986). Some data was reported for 54 offenders, 30 of whom had completed a programme. Specifically, increases of between 25 per cent and 90 per cent in alcohol knowledge was reported – 32 per cent cut down their drinking to a level within their personal targets, and 36 per cent reduced their overall consumption. Although this study did not include a control group, modest improvements were reported for offenders who completed the programme; the data on effectiveness have indicated: 'a slightly lower reconviction rate for compulsory attenders' (Godfrey and Leahy 1986).

The first Alcohol Education Course in Scotland was based on a group of 10 offenders referred from the Dundee courts, who completed a course in 1981, although no formal evaluation was planned, and no follow-up data are available (Robertson and Heather 1982). The course was based on information about alcohol, and some behavioural methods for reducing drinking/ offending behaviours. The court service was not continued, due to problems with system maintenance, and this work was terminated in Dundee in 1982.

Despite discontinuation of this service in Dundee, the same model was transferred to Forfar (Angus) during 1981. A similar service was established by a senior social worker to provide a referral service for the Sheriff (High) courts. Offenders with drink-related offending behaviours attended an Alcohol Education Course as a condition of a probation order (Baldwin, Ford, and Heather 1987; Baldwin, Ford, Heather, and Braggins 1987). Despite the completion of eighteen courses since 1981, however, no systematic follow-up has been completed, and data on effectiveness have not been collected.

Another service in Dumbarton, Scotland, has reported findings for follow-ups of individual offenders with alcohol problems (Tate 1985; Collins and Tate 1988). Although the agency has not provided Alcohol Education Courses for offenders, an individual- and group-counselling service has been offered to persons referred from District (Magistrates) courts. Data on effectiveness has suggested that of 29 offenders who received counselling between 1981 and 1987, 24 had not reoffended at 6 months follow-up. At 36 months follow-up, 15 of these persons had not reoffended. Overall, the findings suggested that 83 per cent of persons who accepted counselling did not reoffend during their period of deferment and 62 per cent of their group did not reoffend during the subsequent 24 months (Collins and Tate 1988). No control group was included, however.

A recent review of UK alcohol education initiatives reported questionnaire data from twenty agencies (Baldwin and Heather 1987). Ninety per cent of agencies offered courses as a condition of a probation order, whilst some also accepted clients who offended as part of a deferred sentence. The average course length was 12 hours, distributed over 6 sessions. The main aim of 10 agencies (50 per cent) was to provide 'education': 6 other agencies (30 per cent) stated that the main aim was behaviour change by offenders. Examination of course contents suggested that: all AECs included group discussions; 95 per cent included drink diaries; 90 per cent included health education materials. Since the first course in 1981, at least 240 separate courses had been completed, with more than 1,950 'graduates' of these courses.

An update of this review has extended the original study, and confirmed many of its findings (Cochrane *et al*. 1989). This review was based on information collected from 55 UK agencies. Comparison between the two reviews of UK agencies which offered AEC services suggest specific trends in service development. In particular:

1. The statutory sector, Probation, Social Work and Social Services Departments have retained 80 per cent involvement in national service provision.

2. Alcohol Education Courses have been directed at younger offenders, mostly aged between 17 and 29.

3. The courses generally have not been made available for female offenders.

4. There has been more use of deferred sentencing by courts.

5. A trend towards shorter courses has occurred (reduction by 25 per cent of average length).

6. The emphasis has continued on 'education' (i.e. provision of information about alcohol), rather than the acquisition of skills.

7. The mean number of offenders who have completed Alcohol Education Courses has been similar in both studies – 7.29 offenders per course in 1986; 7.23 offenders per AEC in 1988.

8. The percentage of agencies expressing a commitment to evaluation has remained constant (85 per cent).

9. The number using controlled evaluations to investigate the effectiveness of courses has remained constant (0 per cent).

The Dundee project was based on the original alcohol education model developed during a previous attempt to establish court-based service provision. The original model was, however, modified to account for more recent developments in social work theory and social psychology (McGuire and Priestley 1985). In particular, the programme was adapted to included specific skill-teaching components on 'not offending', strategies for 'going straight', as well as a focus on skills in abstinence or controlled drinking.

The course was designed to run for 6 weekly sessions, each lasting 2 hours. It was based on verbal presentation of materials by a course tutor, with use of audiovisual aids. Sessions involved minimal use of didactic methods, with a focus on self-help and self-learning by participants. Group discussions were used to enable peer learning where appropriate and the revised programme has been published as a training pack for alcohol educators (Baldwin *et al.* 1988).

The rationale for the revised contents was based on several factors, which included:

1. Evidence for the effectiveness of action-based strategies for this specific client group (Prochaska and Diclemente 1986).

2. The need to produce materials specifically for problem behaviours of the client group in relation to overdrinking and offending (Blackburn 1980).

3. The provision of direct assistance through skills teaching for problem behaviours (McGuire and Priestley 1985).

4. The modification of behaviour via skills teaching, in addition to information provision (Heather and Robertson 1983a; Robertson and Heather 1982).

5. A focus on the direct modification of specific behaviours, for example, via contingency management and self-monitoring procedures rather than on general concepts such as 'alcoholic' (Stumphauzer 1986).

6. Inclusion of principles such as self-recording methods derived from previous research in behaviour therapy and self-control training (Stumphauzer and Perez 1982).

7. Use of behavioural contracting to promote compliance, including: (a) details of privileges which would follow responsible behaviours; (b) details of the responsibilities required to secure privileges; (c) a system of sanctions for failure to meet responsibilities; (d) bonus provision for compliance behaviours (Stuart 1971).

The rationale also was based on more general assumptions about the efficacy of brief behavioural interventions with client populations and other beliefs about the efficacy of group-based interventions with juvenile and young adult offenders.

The controlled evaluation research project in Dundee was the first attempt to measure the effectiveness of Alcohol Education Courses in field settings. Whilst the ideal experimental design would have incorporated random allocation to a no-intervention (or waiting list) 'control' group, a complex field setting which involved: (1) courts; (2) social workers; and (3) non-statutory services prevented the use of this strategy.

Implementation of the Alcohol Education Course package required co-ordination between staff and workers in several unconnected agencies. Successful implementation of the package thus was contingent on the co-operation and integration of workers in discrete service systems with no previous linkages. Therefore, whilst course implementation was based on a design to meet evaluation research criteria, the views, needs, and preferences of local 'stakeholders' (including social workers and social work managers) also were obtained. This approach, consistent with principles of 'action research' was a deliberate strategy to involve the full range of local personnel, including social workers who would be involved in subsequent service provision. The eventual evaluation design was thus modified by this process of consultation with local agencies. The implementation process was consistent with the requirements for the local development of alcohol services between statutory and non-statutory agencies (Tether and Robinson 1986).

This concludes our examination of Alcohol Education Courses, the role of minimal interventions, and controlled drinking. We have considered also a variety of helping styles in working with problem drinkers and the importance of assessment and goal setting, primarily drawing upon the work of social learning theorists. At an earlier point in the chapter we had emphasised the significance of relapse in working with problem drinkers.

In the next chapter Rosemary Kent will focus upon social workers' attitudes to female drinkers in the context of women's vulnerable place in society as a whole. Rosemary Kent examines the ambivalence felt by both female clients and social workers when examining drinking problems – the conflicts and barriers to the behavioural change they are seeking. The chapter goes on to examine various aspects of alcohol-related problems in women and makes some suggestions for more effective intervention by social workers.

© 1990 Steve Baldwin

References

Bailey, H. and Purser, R. (1982) *Coventry Alcohol Education Group*, West Midlands Probation Service, Coventry.

Baldwin, S. (1987) 'Working with people who have alcohol problems', training video, University of Dundee.

Baldwin, S., Ford, I., and Heather, N. (1987) 'Drink and Crime I', *Community Care* 2 April, pp. 12–13.

Baldwin, S., Ford, I., Heather, N., and Braggins, F. (1987) 'Drink and Crime II', *Community Care* 9 April, pp. 22–3.

Baldwin, S. and Heather, N. (1987) 'Alcohol education courses and offenders: a survey of UK agencies, *Alcohol and Alcoholism*.

Baldwin, S., Wilson, M., Lancaster, A., and Allsop, D. (1988) 'Ending offending: an alcohol resource pack for people working with young offenders', Scottish Council on Alcohol, Glasgow.

Bandura, A. (1977) 'Self-efficacy: toward a unifying theory of behaviour change', *Psychological Review* 84:191–215.

Bergin, A.E. (1980) 'Negative effects revisited: a reply', *Professional Psychology* 11:93–100.

Blackburn, R. (1980) 'Still not working? A look at recent outcomes in offender rehabilitation', paper presented at the Scottish branch of the British Psychological Society on deviance, University of Stirling.

Clement, S. (1987) *An Evaluation of the Salford CAT*, London: DHSS.

Cochrane, S., Baldwin, S., Greer, C., and McCluskey, S. (1989) 'Alcohol education courses and offenders: an update on UK services', *Alcohol and Alcoholism* (in press).

Collins, S.A. and Tate, D.H. (1988) 'Alcohol-related offenders and a voluntary organisation in a Scottish community', *The Howard Journal of Criminal Justice* 27(1):44–57.

Corden, J. and Preston-Shoot, M. (1988) *Contracts in Social Work*, Aldershot: Gower.

Davies, D.L. (1962) 'Normal drinking in recovered alcohol addicts', *Quarterly Journal of the Studies on alcohol* 23:94–104.

Diclemente, C.C. and Prochaska, J.D. (1982) 'Self-change and therapy of smoking behaviour: a comparison of processor of change and maintenance', *Addictive Behaviour* 7:133–42.

Egan, G. (1986) *The Skilled Helper*, Monterey: Brooks/Cole.

Godfrey, R. and Leahy, N. (1986) 'Education with the probation service', *Alcohol Concern* 2 March (8):17–19.

Heather, N. (1986) 'Minimal treatment interventions for problem drinkers', in G. Edwards (ed.) *Current Issues in Clinical Psychology*, vol. 4, New York: Plenum.

Heather, N. and Robertson, I. (1983a) *Controlled Drinking*, revised edn, London: Methuen.

Heather, N. and Robertson, I. (1983b) 'Why is abstinence necessary for the recovery of some problem drinkers?' *British Journal of Addiction* 78:139–44.

Heron, J. (1975) 'Six category intervention analysis', Human Potential Research Project, University of Surrey.

McConnaughty, E., Prochaska, J.O., Velicer, W., and Diclemente, C.C. (1984) Replication of the stages of change in psychotherapy', unpublished manuscript, University of Rhode Island.

McGuire, J. and Priestly, P. (1985) *Offending Behaviour: Skills and Strategies for Going Straight*, London: Batsford.

McMurran, M. (1988) *There's No Booze Behind Bars*, London: Home Office.

Mahoney, J. (1974) *Cognition and Behaviour Modification*, Cambridge, Massachusetts: Ballinger.

Marlatt, G.A. (1979) 'Craving for alcohol, loss of control and relapse: a cognitive behavioural analysis', in P.E. Nathan, G.A. Marlatt, and T. Lobog (eds) *Alcoholism: New Directions in Behavioural Research and Treatment*, New York: Plenum.

Marlatt, G.A. and Gordon, J.R. (1980) 'Determinants of relapse: implications for the maintenance of behaviour change', in P.O. Davidson and S.M. Davidson (eds) *Behavioural Medicine: Changing Health Lifestyles*, New York: Brunner/Mazel.

Marlatt, G.A. and Gordon, J.R. (1985) *Relapse Prevention*, New York: Guildford Press.

Marlatt, G.A. and Parks, G.A. (1982) 'Self management of addictive behaviours', in P. Karoly and F.H. Kanfer (eds) *Self Management and Behaviour Change*, New York: Pergamon.

Menary, R. (1986) *Alcohol Education Programmes for Offenders*, Taunton: Somerset Probation Service.

Miller, W.R. (1983) 'Motivational interviewing with problem drinkers', *Behavioural Psychotherapy* 11:147–72.

Miller, W.R., Sovereign, R.G., and Krege, B. (1988) 'Motivational interviewing with problem drinkers II: the drinker's check up as a preventive intervention', *Behavioural Psychotherapy* 16:125–68.

Miller, W.R. and Taylor, C.A. (1980) 'Relative effectiveness of bibliotherapy, individual and group self-control training in the treatment of problem drinkers', *Addictive Behaviours* 15:13–24.

Northamptonshire Probation Service (1982) *Corby Alcohol Therapy Group (1979–81)*, Report, Northampton.

Pattison, E.M. (1976) 'Non-abstinent drinking goals in the treatment of alcoholism', *Archives of General Psychiatry* 33:923–30.

Prochaska, J.O. and Diclemente, C.C. (1982) 'Transtheoretical therapy: toward a more integrative model of change', *Psychotherapy: Theory, Research and Practice* 19:276–8.

Prochaska, J.O. and Diclemente, C.C. (1983) 'Stages and processes of self-change of smoking: toward an integrative model of change', *Journal of Consulting and Clinical Psychology* 51:390–5.

Prochaska, J.O. and Diclemente, C.C. (1986) 'Towards a comprehensive model of change' in H. Heather and W.R. Miller (eds) *Treating Addictive Behaviours: Process of Change*, New York: Plenum Press.

Robertson, I. and Heather, N. (1982) 'An alcohol education course for young offenders: a preliminary report', *British Journal on Alcohol and Alcoholism* 17:32–8.

Shapiro, S.B. (1968) 'Some aspects of a theory of interpersonal contracts', Psychological Reports 23:171–83.

Singer, L.R. (1983) *Trouble through drink: An evaluation of the Reading Alcohol Study Group*, Reading: Berkshire Probation Service.

Strupp, H.H., Hadley, S.W., and Gomer-Schwartz, B. (1977) *Psycho-*

therapy for Better or Worse: The Problem of Negative Effects, New York: Jason Aronson.

Stuart, R.B. (1971) 'Behavioural contracting within the families of delinquents', *Journal of Behaviour Therapy and Experimental Psychiatry* 2:1–11.

Stumphauzer, J.S. (1986) *Helping Delinquent Change*, New Brunswick, New Jersey: Transaction Books.

Stumphauzer, J.S. and Perez, P. (1982) 'Learning not to drink II: peer survey of normal adolescents', *International Journal of the Addictions* 17(8):1363–73.

Tate, D. (1985) 'New ventures: an offer of help to alcohol-related offenders', *Bulletin of Scottish Legal Action Group*, March, 38–9.

Tether, P. and Robinson, D. (1986) *Preventing Alcohol Problems: A Guide to Local Action*, London: Tavistock.

Vogler, R.E., Compton, J.V., and Weissbach, J.A. (1976) 'The referral problem in the field of alcohol abuse', *Journal of Community Psychology* 4:357–61.

Wollersheim, J.P., McFall, M.E., Hamilton, S.B., Hickey, C.S., and Borderwick, M.C. (1980) 'Effects of treatment rationale and problem severity on perceptions of psychological problems and counselling approaches', *Journal of Counselling Psychology* 27:225–31.

Chapter four

Focusing on women

Rosemary Kent

The clients of most generic social workers are women and children. In contrast, the tradition of 'working with alcoholics' has implied dealing with men. Much that has been written in the research and treatment literature has assumed that it is male drinking patterns and ensuing difficulties which need to be better understood. The equation that 'alcoholic' clients equals male clients may be one of the crucial but often overlooked aspects of why the social work profession has remained hesitant to respond very readily to alcohol problems. In recent years, the terms 'alcoholic' and 'alcoholism' have been de-emphasised in favour of a broader conceptualisation of drink-related problems, and an increasing number of studies have linked regular heavy or dependent drinking to common presenting problems in social work caseloads (see Chapter 2) and yet, many social workers still assume that only a small proportion of their clients drink in a manner that causes harm – simply because their caseload is mainly female, or family-orientated.

At the same time as the role of social workers in recognising and dealing with alcohol problems is being highlighted, there is also a gradual increase in trying to understand the specific drinking patterns and problems of women. This chapter discusses the importance of bringing these trends together – and in particular, tackling some of the underlying difficulties in changing our traditional assumptions, attitudes, and approaches to women whose drinking is problematic.

Theories about women and drinking

Why has there only recently been the recognition that helping people with alcohol-related problems needs to *include* helping women?

First, women are drinking considerably more in Britain than they have in previous generations. In England and Wales, there was no significant change in male drinkers' consumption between 1978 and 1987, whereas women's drinking increased significantly – from 4.8 to 6 units per week on average amongst 25–34 year-olds, and from 4.6 to 6.1 units per week amongst 35–44 year-olds (Goddard and Ikin 1988). A survey on drinking and attitudes to licensing in Scotland, carried out on behalf of the OPCS, 'found that the consumption of alcohol by women aged between 26–45 rose by one-third in the period 1976–1984' (Social Work Services Group 1987:3). The proportion of mothers with young children who drink rose from 24 per cent in 1930 to 91 per cent in 1971 (Robinson 1988).

Although their per capita consumption remains well below that of men, there have been commercial and social pressures which have ensured that women increase their drinking to a level which is exploitable in the market place, and reflects the so-called liberation of women which the 1960s and 1970s heralded. In fact, the rapid change in the availability of alcohol for women has meant that the attitudes of society have not always kept pace, and women's apparent freedom of choice is often undermined by overt and subtle social pressures. Commercial interests promote the idea that women are entirely reponsible for when, where, what, and how much they drink, but tradition dies hard: society has not yet got used to the idea that some women may drink heavily – indeed, they may drink 'like men'.

Alcohol is much cheaper today, in real terms, than it was in the 1950s (Hunt 1982). Consumption doubled between 1950 and 1980, and the most dramatic increases have been in the sale of wine, and spirits such as vodka, gin, and white rum, which are often marketed as 'women's drinks' (Shaw 1980). Women have much more disposable income than in the 1960s and before, even though many of their jobs are low paid and/or part-time (McConville 1983). There have been changes in patterns of employment: for instance in 1963, 60 per cent of those working in pubs and clubs were women, whilst in 1978 there were 68 per cent. This constitutes a total of 245,000 women and is significant, as involvement in the production and selling of alcohol is a high-risk factor in the likelihood of heavy drinking developing. There are more women in jobs which were previously a male preserve, and it is likely that this also results in heavier drinking amongst women in these occupations.

It was during the 1960s and 1970s that there was a lifting of restrictions on women's access to alcohol: women could no longer officially be discriminated against in pubs, and there has been an increase in the number and types of settings which women are likely to frequent where alcohol is served, e.g. wine bars and bars in cinemas. There are many more outlets where women can buy alcohol without any particular stigma – there are numerous 'corner shops' with licences to sell alcohol, and the majority of supermarkets are also licensed to do so. In the 1970s off-licences were permitted to open normal shopping hours and, overall, women are now more important than men as bulk purchasers of alcohol (Shaw 1980).

As well as economic factors, there are social factors encouraging a general increase in women's drinking: advertising is increasingly targeted at particular groups of women, pubs are keen to attract families, and many brewing houses are trying to promote a less 'macho' image in the ambience of their pubs.

Some writers (Keil 1978 and Wilsnack 1976) presented evidence that women in the 1970s were likely to use alcohol to resolve sex-role conflicts and the pressures of combining the role of housewife with that of worker outside the home. There have also been attempts to identify particular stressful life events as being more important precipitants of excessive drinking in women than in men. Cooke and Allan (1984), however, point out that the frequent association of certain transitions or events in a women's life with a possible increase in drinking should not be ignored, but that this may be more characteristic of women in alcohol treatment programmes, and less true for heavy drinkers in the general population. In fact, their own research (a general population study of 230 women in Scotland) showed no evidence that women increase their alcohol consumption in response to life events. They suggest that the life-event hypothesis may have arisen because of the need for a 'special' explanation of heavy drinking by females, given women's relatively low per capita consumption compared to men. Whether or not the reasons for women's transitions from moderate to heavy drinking are on the whole different from men's is still very underresearched.

Another reason for recognising that helping people with alcohol-related problems should include women, is that the increase in alcohol-related problems in women is occurring more rapidly than the proportional increase in male problems. Statistics show marked and sudden increases in various indicators of harm linked to drinking, e.g. drunkenness offences, liver cirrhosis mortality, deaths from 'alcoholism' and alcoholic psychosis, and drink-driving offences. The number of women receiving treatment and/or attending self-help groups is also increasing more rapidly amongst women than amongst men.

Robinson points out:

On average, women weigh 15 per cent less than men. It follows that the smaller a body, the less the body fluid, the more concentrated a given amount of alcohol will be, and the more intoxicated one feels and the more harm the toxicity of alcohol will inflict.

(Robinson 1988:57)

Also, a given amount of alcohol will be concentrated in a smaller amount of body fluid in a woman than in a man of exactly the same weight. Thus the liver is particularly vulnerable to the ravages of alcohol, resulting in scarring, hepatitis, cirrhosis, and cancers. In Britain, women are very nearly as likely as men to die of cirrhosis, whilst in almost every other country in which such records are available, the rate of cirrhosis mortality amongst women is one-tenth to one-half of the rate for men. The reasons for this are little understood (Robinson 1988). There is some risk of cirrhosis at two or three standard drinks per day for women (four for men) and a high risk for women who drink about five standard drinks per day (Royal College of Psychiatrists 1986).

In fact, there are many harms to individuals and society which are associated with high levels of alcohol consumption, but not many of them have been widely or systematically researched in terms of gender differences. It may well be that there are hidden links between increases in family dysfunction, psychiatric problems, various physical illnesses, and particular criminal offences, and the rise in the per capita consumption of women in the last twenty years.

A third area in which there is a greater interest than in the past in women and drinking, is the recognition that when women experience types of problems which are different to those experienced by men, they may need different types of help. Many traditional approaches claim to be gender neutral, insisting that the similarities of harm and distress experienced by women and men are more numerous and important than the differences. It appears that North America is considerably further ahead than we are in Britain in highlighting the special needs of women drinkers, and implementing treatment programmes which are both popular and effective. Writers such as Kalant (1980), Burtle (1979), and Wilsnack and Beckman (1984) have put together the theory, research, and examples of intervention which are influential in helping women with drinking problems across the Atlantic. There are also interesting autobiographical and journalistic accounts, such as Sandmaier's *The Invisible Alcoholics* (1980). In Britain, books by Camberwell Council on Alcoholism (1980), McConville

(1983), Robinson (1988), and Kent (1989) have focused on the ways in which the context of women's drinking, and many of its consequences, is unique to their gender. A conference on 'Women's Problems with Alcohol and Other Drugs: Improving our Response' (Waterson *et al.* 1986) was held in 1986 in England, and Drugs Alcohol Women Nationally (DAWN) has campaigned and produced publications to raise awareness of women's issues, drawing particular attention to the position of black women *vis-à-vis* drinking and help with drinking problems. Research projects and descriptions of good-quality projects to address women's needs are still comparatively rare in Britain, and very few are published in the established journals.

A fourth aspect of the recent, gradual interest in women's drinking is the exploration of the social and political context of a number of 'women's issues'. Women's powerlessness in relation to health, social work and criminal justice systems is highlighted in such books as Hutter and Williams (1981) *Controlling Women: The Normal and the Deviant*, Brook and Davis (1985) *Women, The Family and Social Work*, and Evans and Ungerson (1983) *Sexual Divisions: Patterns and Processes*. A structural analysis of excessive drinking in women tends to regard it as parallel to smoking, eating disorders, and illicit drug use. The same socio-cultural pressures are likely to contribute to the development of all these patterns of behaviour (see, for example, MacLennan 1976; Wolfson and Murray 1986). These may be attempts at rebellion and escape, providing relief or comfort in the short-term, but containing also a self-destructive element which must be understood in the context of women's undervalued position in society.

Vulnerability

Women who are clients of social work agencies may be vulnerable to problem drinking at a higher rate than women in the general population. Shaw *et al.* (1978) found that heavy drinkers were three times more likely to have visited a 'helping agency' than moderate or non-drinkers. Men are more likely than women to have their families cover up the consequences of their drinking, and the behaviour of a male parent is less likely to cause concern about the welfare of children, than is the behaviour of a mother. Alcohol is a relatively cheap, legal, easily available, and quick-acting psychic painkiller, and is therefore a common way of coping with or escaping from all sorts of distress. When this distress is chronic, women (more often than men) are likely to seek help from others – either their family, or health, welfare, or psychological services.

Alternatively, intervention may be imposed on a woman, under the guise of 'help', if her distress is being seen to have an adverse effect on her children. This is particularly noticeable if the client is a drug user or heavy drinker.

At the time of contact with professional helpers, including social workers, moderate or heavy drinking may be a major support to the drinker. It may be more beneficial than harmful to her, or on the other hand, her drinking pattern may in subtle or obvious ways be perpetuating or adding to the cause of her distress. The helper needs to understand the woman's subjective experience of drinking and the functions it has, as well as endeavouring to identify the consequences of the drinking in an objective sense. Many women will continue to rely on alcohol to 'get by', unless the social worker introduces drinking as a legitimate topic of discussion. This will be most evident if the drinker is unaware of connections between the pattern of her drinking and the harm or distress that she is being helped with. It is interesting to note that a report by Mintel in 1987 found that 64 per cent of men who were moderate drinkers did not think that alcohol affected health, whereas 70 per cent of women had this belief.

Social workers are likely to be called upon to intervene in circumstances which may be causes and/or consequences of excessive drinking, for instance, bereavement, domestic violence, relationship difficulties, problems in parenting, sexual abuse, and mental and physical ill-health. Drinking may be a way of dulling the emotions stirred up in the woman, emotions which are not readily tolerated in our culture – such as resentment, anger, hopelessness, or rebellion. Alcohol is also a way of avoiding conflict, and escaping the sense of failure when conflicts constantly recur. For instance, it appears that women are often caught by economic necessity in the trap of living with a violent partner (see Orford 1975). It is also more likely that women will start drinking heavily to keep up with the excessive drinking of a male partner, than vice versa.

Many drinkers, including social work clients, are not likely to be aware of when the 'therapeutic' effects of alcohol begin to be outweighed by the problems that it causes. A non-judgemental and informative response by the social worker to the possibility that a client's drinking is heavy, can be an extremely productive, straightforward intervention. The unwillingness of many social workers to address how much their clients drink, and what consequences it has, seems to be connected to beliefs that social workers have about why women turn to drink. Social workers need to be clear about their attitudes, avoiding slipping into the role of either 'rescuer' or 'persecutor'.

The individual social worker may consciously or unconsciously identify with the client, believing that her experience of drinking alcohol must be very similar to their own. The social worker will have views about the apparent rationality or irrationality of the heavy drinker, and may avoid a constructive approach to helping the woman with her individual problem. For instance, the helper may say: 'I'm not surprised she drinks heavily – I don't blame her, I'd probably do the same in her situation. Anyway she's got nothing to put in its place, has she?' It is important for the social worker to recognise both the broader political context, and the personal situation of the drinker, and to facilitate her coping with and emerging from the vulnerable position she is in. In other circumstances, the social worker may ignore the context of the woman's drinking, and become totally mystified by a pattern of behaviour which seems to have obvious and serious harmful consequences. The temptation, then, is for the social worker to 'admit defeat', to regard the drinker as having gone beyond the bounds of what can be understood and therefore effectively dealt with. In both examples the social worker imposes beliefs about why heavy drinking occurs with insufficient attention to the client's uniqueness. The female client's vulnerability to developing alcohol problems should contribute to a respectful and alert response, but should not be a way of avoiding recognition of the client's personal responsibility for making changes.

Ambivalence – in the social worker and the client

There is considerable ambivalence towards problem drinkers within British society as a whole, so that we all tend to feel a mixture of pity, mistrust, disapproval, and concern, in varying degrees. There is further confusion for the social worker in that with the de-medicalisation of 'alcoholism', the helping professions are no longer encouraged to see irrational drinking behaviour as being caused by an illness called alcoholism. Shaw *et al.* (1978) have discussed some of the psychological mechanisms that primary care workers use to avoid acknowledging or dealing with alcohol problems (see Chapter 3). When it comes to women's drinking, society has clearly defined opinions about when, where, and how much women should drink, opinions about women who get drunk, and opinions about those women whose drinking has an adverse affect on others, mainly their families. It is inevitable that this mixture of feelings and expectations is going to interfere when social workers aim to help clients who have been harmed by their drinking.

Many writers (such as McConville 1983) have pointed out that heavy expectations are placed on women to be society's moral custodians, and to sacrifice themselves for the general wellbeing of their husbands and children. The extreme disinhibition of being drunk threatens the image of female purity. Drunkenness is often equated with promiscuity, and the repeated inability of a woman to control her drinking is seen as a total opting-out of the female role (Kent 1989). What seems most unacceptable to society is that something as apparently pleasurable (and also selfish) as drinking alcohol should replace the selflessness which is regarded as some kind of 'natural' female characteristic. The heavy drinker who fails to take care of how she looks is assumed to have lost her self-respect, which society quickly interprets as her having no right to be treated with respect. If a woman's willingness or capacity to care for others and for herself disappears, it assumes that she has become nothing.

Such harsh attitudes are obviously in conflict with the conscious approach of most social workers. The social work task is to help, to take a non-judgemental attitude and to find, with the client, ways of overcoming hardship or crisis. It is often difficult for social workers to retain a sense of 'unconditional positive regard', or neutrality. In dealing with a woman who apparently cannot or will not control her drinking, the busy social worker may well give in to negative feelings about her. He or she may try to help, whilst at the same time trying to avoid having to identify the client as 'a woman who drinks too much'. Both client and worker are likely to find it more comfortable to avoid talking about drinking, unless there is a crisis, at which point the role of alcohol can no longer be ignored. This ambivalence, which is very common in the helper and in the self-image of a woman drinker, can be overcome as workers and clients get more practice in seeing drinking patterns as a legitimate topic for discussion.

Isaacs and Moon (1985) studied the attitudes and response of a sample of social workers in a local authority office and identified a number of ambivalences in perceptions and in managing alcohol-related problems. Some of their respondents argued strongly that 'the sex of a client had no influence on the identification of the problem or the response given by a social worker' (Isaacs and Moon 1985). However, the authors found a general trend which suggested that alcohol problems in women were less acceptable and less tolerable. Links between drinking and sexual promiscuity were made, and 'women's alcohol problems were viewed severely at least in part because of their effect on a woman's ability to look after children' (Isaacs and Moon 1985:25). In a detailed analysis of case notes, it was found that out of 54 problem drinkers, 31 were female.

Rosemary Kent

Child safety and/or self-neglect were the most frequent reasons for the problem drinking becoming a concern of the Social Services Department. The responses the social workers made to their drinking clients was on the whole a holding operation, bringing in a third party or focusing on the welfare of the children. There appears to have been very little direct work with the client about addressing the possibility of changing their behaviour.

The social workers described themselves as being either tactful or authoritarian in raising the topic of a possible change in the client's drinking habits. Both in the questionnaire, and in the vignettes of five case studies, Isaacs and Moon point to the ambivalence of the social workers in their attitudes and in their ways of working with problem drinkers. The majority of them had come across plenty of alcohol-related problems in their professional lives, but had very little training in how to deal with these, and relatively few of the respondents had developed any great interest in problems of alcohol abuse.

The social work response

A helpful way for social workers to retain a non-judgemental and less confused approach to women with drinking problems, is to focus on the three overlapping areas in which they may be called upon to intervene. In Chapter 1 it has been noted that drinking can lead to harm because of intoxication, because of regular, heavy use, or because of the phenomenon of 'alcohol dependence'.

Attitudes to intoxication

As has been noted, attitudes to drunkenness in women tend to be markedly different from views of drunkenness in men. David Ennals, Secretary of State for Social Services, said in 1978 at the opening of a campaign on alcohol education: 'there is really nothing manly or heroic or glamorous about those who drink too much. In men it is crude and embarrassing: in women it is plain sickening'. Indeed, many people assume that even worse than an intoxicated woman, is an intoxicated mother. It is assumed that she is likely to abuse her children or act irresponsibly whilst they are with her. What little evidence we have indicates that whilst it is possible that a mother may on some occasions whilst drunk ignore a child's immediate needs, it is more common for her to allow herself to get drunk only whilst her children are asleep or out of the house (Mayer and Black 1977). Our alarm about the unsteady, drunk figure of a woman in a public place – statistically a rare sight

– tends inappropriately to colour our expectations of what *could* happen if a woman is drunk whilst children are in her care. Intoxication may, in a sense, be more of a problem for the worker than for the client: it may lead to revulsion, panic, or fantasies of gross irresponsibility. If a client is seen to be intoxicated, or rumours are heard about her getting drunk, the social worker may rush to take some kind of action in haste, without exploring such factors as the frequency of the intoxication, the part it plays in the client's family as a whole, or the extent of harm – if any – it causes to herself and those around her.

This is not to say that there are no dangers involved in a woman being drunk. If she drinks very large amounts, she will be causing both acute and possibly long-term physical harm. She could also cause harm to others, for instance, by setting something alight through carelessness. But to keep things in proportion, it should be remembered that:

1. Women are less often drunk than men, and it is single, childless women and men who drink more and are therefore more often drunk than mothers (Breeze 1985).

2. Anecdotal evidence indicates that many mothers restrict their periods of intoxication to times when children will be less affected.

3. Many women who drink large amounts frequently, may have a high level of tolerance to alcohol, which means that they are able to carry out day-to-day responsibilities, even with a high blood–alcohol level – often without appearing to be drunk. This is known as functional tolerance.

Recognising regular, heavy use of alcohol

This should concern the social worker both with regard to the well-being of the client herself, and the welfare of those close to her. Again the helper needs to be on guard against a moralistic or punitive attitude. Their energy needs to be directed towards understanding the drinker's behaviour in the context of her life as a whole, and in working with the client to identify the pros and cons of her drinking pattern. The social worker also needs to make a careful assessment of the degree of difficulty the client might experience in changing the pattern, and how ready she is (if at all) to try to make these changes. The worker must be aware of existing or potential alcohol-related harms, and should provide the client with detailed and accurate information about this. 'Shock–horror' statements such as 'Your children could be taken away from you' and other threats, should be avoided. It is, however, appropriate for the client to be given a realistic account of the possible consequences of her drinking by the social worker, and the client should be given details of exactly what would be required of her for these consequences to be removed.

Understanding alcohol dependence

'Degree of dependence' has been defined as the degree of discomfort a person experiences in the absence of a substance or activity (Russell 1975). When considering dependence on alcohol or other drugs, we usually imply that some harm is occurring, but it is very often regular, heavy use which is the harm that has brought the client to the attention of Social Services, rather than the specific 'dependency' characteristics.

If we examine our attitudes to women who are severely dependent on alcohol, we may find that we take an extreme stance. Either we pity them because they are weak, helpless, and in need of rescuing, or we focus on the harm that is occurring, and brush aside the distress or struggle which makes behaviour change difficult (i.e. the main element of dependence). The dangers inherent in adopting the former attitude is that a stereotype of women as passive and inadequate is perpetuated, the drinker may not be allowed or encouraged to take responsibility for her own behaviour, and she may be manipulated (unconsciously) into transferring her dependence onto the social worker. This encourages the notion of dependence as some inherent 'female characteristic'. The dangers of the other extreme – of focusing on the overt problems resulting from her drinking – is that women are stereotyped as irrational and irresponsible, or as intrinsically more pathological than men (see Broverman *et al.* 1970). The social worker may then become impatient and punitive. It is not uncommon for social workers to veer from one extreme to the other, particularly if the client's behaviour triggers different needs or psychological projections in the worker at different times. As has been noted in Chapter 5, the roles of rescuer and persecutor may be adopted by the social worker. Claude Steiner (1979) has used a Transactional Analysis approach to illustrate the shifting roles associated with problem drinkers, adopted by both helpers and drinkers themselves. Both will take the role of rescuer, persecutor, and victim at different times in their relationship as drinking episodes stop and start, and it is not until the 'game' is exposed, that an adult relationship can be established, and lasting change achieved.

In discussing the attitudes and mixed feelings of the worker towards the alcohol-dependent woman, we also need to consider how the client may herself experience a mass of conflicting emotions and assumptions. Even if she is aware of the harms caused by her drinking, she will feel ambivalent about her behaviour. She is likely to feel that she can't live without alcohol, yet she hates its power over her. She can't imagine facing the world without a drink, but she is ashamed of what people think of her because she drinks. She may want things to change, but she may not be convinced that it is her drinking habits that need changing. In addition to this, she will experience conflicting demands and expectations from people around her, for instance: 'You could easily cut down your drinking if you really wanted to', or 'You're an alcoholic – you can't help it', or 'You should get out and meet people more, then you wouldn't need to drink so much'. Another source of stress for her may be confusion about whether her drinking would automatically decrease if she resolved particular problems in her life, for instance, if she left her husband, or if she moved house.

Both men and women experience these areas of ambivalence and conflict to some extent. Amongst female problem drinkers, however, the messages they receive both directly and indirectly from family, friends, and professionals may be more strongly guilt-inducing. Many of these messages may have been inculcated long before the drinking started, laid down in 'scripts' about 'proper' female behaviour, what women should and shouldn't feel, and what they should expect. A woman, we are told, should be passive and accommodating, but if her circumstances become overwhelmingly difficult and she becomes depressed, she is defined as being inadequate. If she becomes angry or makes her concerns public, she is regarded as being unfeminine. Women are expected to take emotional responsibility for all those close to them. Gender stereotyping is sufficiently powerful in out culture that most women internalise these expectations. It is important for those in a helping role to avoid perpetuating inappropriate and damaging expectations, which will contribute to the conflicts and distress that the alcohol-dependent woman is likely to be experiencing.

Conflicts and barriers

In direct work with the woman who has drink-related problems, there are three main areas in which both the client and her social worker may experience conflict, ambivalence and barriers. These are, in discussing drinking habits, access to appropriate help, and the need for the client to make changes in her life.

Rosemary Kent

Discussing drinking

Initiating the topic of drinking is a delicate business. Very often professional helpers rely on information from a referral letter or a third party, rather than finding out in the first instance from the client herself. Social workers tend to believe that they do not have the right to ask about clients' drinking habits, and they assume that unless clients themselves volunteer the information, they will not be prepared to talk honestly about drinking (Shaw *et al.* 1978). The social worker may well recognise that it ought to be discussed, but fears that once out in the open it will be too difficult to handle. When working with a woman who the social worker believes might be experiencing difficulties with her drinking, the worker may be very nervous about the response she may make if questioned. The relationship between client and worker may be seen as fragile, with the worker desperately hoping that the client feels secure and trusted but not, in fact, being able to convey this sense of trust to the client. The worker may expect a woman client who drinks to be evasive or to lie. The client in her turn, may be aware of what the social worker is thinking and may reflect the unspoken feeling that the details of her drinking habits are best left undiscussed.

On another level, many drinkers do surreptitiously hope that someone, some time, might recognise that her drinking is excessive, but she also wants acknowledgement that it is scary to talk about it. She will expect to be criticised, but she will automatically insist to anyone who 'confronts' her that there is nothing to be critical of. Part of her acknowledges that there are problems in her life which could be linked to drinking, whilst another part of her strenuously denies this. Another aspect of avoiding the subject because of anticipated criticism is that many clients will, not unnaturally, fear the power of the social worker. They will assume that the social worker is only interested in the harm that her drinking could cause, and therefore will find a way of forcing her to stop drinking, or punishing her, if she does not. If she has children, her overriding fear may be that they will be taken away from her (Thom 1986).

Sometimes the topic of drinking is not ever discussed because neither the client nor the social worker are aware of possible links between the client's alcohol consumption and her presenting problems – whether these are of a practical, physical, or emotional nature. Social workers should alert their clients to the connections that may exist between drinking habits and a wide range of familiar problems. This can be introduced in a general, informative way, without making assumptions that these connections exist for this particular woman. For instance, it is often helpful to talk about the ways in which people might seek to relieve stresses in their life, and to mention that drinking is one of those ways of relaxing which can be useful and appropriate in some circumstances, but troublesome in other circumstances. It is essential that the social worker should show clearly that 'turning to drink' is a very understandable action for many women to take, and that it is very hard to believe, for many of us, that it can cause problems as well as apparently solving them.

Access to appropriate help

Having made it possible for a client to talk freely about her drinking, identifying for herself its costs and benefits, the social worker should then undertake a careful assessment of the severity of drinking, the severity of harm, and the client's readiness to change. The social worker may then make a recommendation, or a formal referral, based on this assessment and the wishes of the client. It may be best for the woman to participate in a self-help group, such as Alcoholics Anonymous, or for her to attend an Alcohol Advice Centre, Treatment Unit, or other specialist agency. There are special difficulties for women when this occurs, partly because there is an implied rejection and, very often, the termination of a relationship. The woman drinker may believe that she is 'too far gone' to be helped by her social worker. She will feel very vulnerable and anxious, particularly if it is the first time anyone has made it possible for her to open up about her drinking. Having lowered her defences and found that she was not instantly dismissed as wicked or crazy, her initial feelings of low self-esteem and mistrust may return, at the point when the social worker raises the question of 'referring on' or 'specialist treatment'. Even though the client may not openly reject the suggestion, she may not be able to identify or talk about her bad feelings. She should be encouraged to express her misgivings, and acknowledge possible hurt, fear, and a sense of rejection. She may also be worried about what will be done with the information she has given to her social worker about her drinking. This period of referral needs to be handled with great sensitivity, as it is often at this point where a woman fails to comply with plans that are made on her behalf, resulting in indignation or anger in the social worker and possibly the agency to which she has been referred. The latter may be quick to place the blame on the drinker herself, and regard her behaviour as justification for withdrawing their help.

As well as the powerful emotions around when a social worker suggests a referral, there are practical and psychological barriers to participation in a specialist treatment or counselling programme. It appears that women are more reluctant to enter formal treatment settings than men, and their structures often discourage women from entering them. This has been discussed by Avon Council on Alcohol in their *Survey of Gateways to Treatment for Women in Avon* (1982) and by Thom (1986), both research projects being prompted by an awareness of the extent to which women are under-represented in many alcohol treatment agencies. Thom's research on women and men attending the out-patient department of an NHS Alcohol Treatment Unit found women were significantly more likely than men to feel that alcohol was not their main problem, and referral to an alcohol clinic was inappropriate. A typical comment was: 'I really feel there is something wrong but I can't pinpoint what . . . I feel I have problems and that makes me drink'. In addition, only one of the married women in the sample reported her husband urging her to accept drinking as the central problem, whereas all of the married men said their wives had made such remarks at some time. Very similar attitudes are held by many social workers and other potential referral agents: for instance the Avon Council on Alcoholism researchers quote this comment as being typical of their social work sample: 'In general I tend to see alcohol abuse as a symptom of stresses in the family, and the focus of my work would be in dealing with the underlying factors within the family relationships' (Avon Council on Alcohol 1982:22). None the less, Thom found in her sample that women and men did not differ significantly in the degree of severity of their alcohol dependence, nor were alcohol-related problems greater for men than for women.

Conflicts can arise between the referring agent, the specialist agency, and the client if there is insufficient clarity about which aspects of the client's life are being addressed or challenged by which person. When there has been Social Services involvement, it is likely that there are many complicated issues within which a client's drinking is embedded, and there should be frequent and thorough liaison between all the agencies involved. The client's responsibility for her own decisions should always be respected – whatever her age, parental, or marital status. The wishes or demands of a client's partner should never be allowed to supersede those of the client herself.

Another potential for conflict between accepting/seeking specialist treatment, and avoiding it, is that women drinkers themselves may regard 'help' as necessary only if their behaviour is harming other people, for instance, their families. It may be difficult for women to accept they have a right to obtaining help on their own behalf. Thom (1986) reports that the women in her research sample emphasised that drinking had not diminished their ability to fulfil their roles as wives and mothers, and therefore there was no need for treatment. This highlights the woman's perception of help or treatment as being some kind of 'correctional' experience, perhaps a re-education to equip her to better perform her female tasks. This may indeed reflect the expectations of the original referring agent. This will obviously be a major barrier for any woman to overcome, if she is to benefit from the opportunity to explore her feelings, choices, and difficulties and change her drinking behaviour.

The client's own priorities may on occasions conflict with those of the social worker. Social Services has statutory responsibilities if a mother is failing in her ability to parent, or if the client is managing her own affairs inadequately and harming others. The conflict between social control and client self-determination is not, of course, unique to social work with problem drinkers. But there are many issues which are thrown into sharp relief when the drinker is a mother, and the social worker is responsible for the children's welfare. By making a referral to a specialist agency, the social worker's expectation might be that this will somehow make the client 'see reason', that she will change her behaviour, and that she will leave that setting 'cured'. A woman drinker may be unwilling or unaware of the need to reduce or stop her alcohol consumption, but pressures on the social worker prevent her from acknowledging this possibility (see Chapters 3 and 6 for discussion of the 'pre-contemplation' stage). The woman may regard her drinking as an antidote to her chronically low self-esteem, for example, and she may regard the resulting neglect of her children as inevitable. The social worker may not have the time, the resources, or the inclination to address properly the spiral of low self-esteem, heavy drinking, poor self-image, and the intervention of Social Services, and may thus make a referral. The fact that the woman is then resentful, confused, resistant to change, and further devoid of self-respect will inevitably mean she is less likely to take and maintain a personal decision to address her drinking.

Many Alcohol Treatment Units in the NHS, and rehabilitation projects run by non-statutory agencies, expect their clients to live in. Many of the longer established treatment facilities are not orientated towards their clients having family responsibilities, and hostels tend to assume that the normal living arrangements of their residents outside are unsatisfactory. Sheehan and Watson (1980) point out that women retain their home-making skills more than men, and are less likely to become homeless. Residential treatment facilities may therefore need to be very attractive for them to want

111

to relinquish their own homes. Most specialist treatment agencies do not offer help with child-care arrangements (DAWN 1986). If a woman normally lives with a partner, the latter will often object to her participating in treatment – if it disrupts life in any way or draws attention to a problem which was previously conveniently hidden. The partner may also encourage the woman to carry on drinking, whilst at the same time criticising her behaviour when intoxicated. These patterns may occur amongst the partners of lesbian drinkers, as well as in male partners. It is less common for home-based men who enter treatment programmes to be under-mined by their partners to the same extent.

Practical problems in attending a counselling or treatment service, may include getting time off from work, or balancing a complicated schedule of home, family, and work responsibilities. Many women in contact with social workers may have difficulties in getting out of the house due to the demands of young children, problems with public transport, or because of agoraphobia or panic attacks. The crippling effect of extreme shame or embarrass-ment should also not be underestimated, and even the most com-mitted help-seeker may not have the courage to turn up at a new agency unless she is given adequate support. The family, sub-culture, or ethnic background of a woman may impose strong taboos against getting help from anyone outside the immediate family. The stigma of making a private problem public – in the sense of sharing it with people other than a doctor or similar professional, may be very great, and many helping agencies may be regarded as only for white people, or only for men, or only for working-class or middle-class people.

There are many conflicting pressures for women drinkers them-selves and for social workers, which interfere with a smooth process of problem identification, followed by referral, followed by resource provision. The temptation to 'send' women clients to some person or agency which 'deals with problem drinkers' needs to be tempered with the recognition of how sensitively such an action must be handled.

The need to make changes

Whether or not a specialist agency is involved in helping the woman problem drinker, the social worker will need to be clear about what changes are required if the client is to establish a more rewarding life, without drinking heavily. Perhaps with a majority of women clients whose difficulties are linked to their drinking, referral will not be needed. The social worker will remain the central 'change agent' and will work with the client on defining and achieving appropriate goals.

There is some danger that the client may draw the worker into a time-consuming exercise of 'if only . . .' in which she argues that if she was rehoused, she wouldn't drink so much, or if only she didn't feel so lonely and depressed, she wouldn't have to turn to the bottle. This is often a serious dilemma for the helper, who may be in two minds about whether to accept the client's view on this, and to try to provide the psychological or practical help required, or whether to insist that a change in the drinking itself should occur first. It may be very difficult to assess what is a prerequisite for the process of personal change to occur, or what would simply be increased cushioning, preventing the client from taking responsibility for the adverse consequences of her drinking. It is sometimes further complicated because of social workers' statutory obligations, particularly with regard to the safety of children.

It is quite possible that neither the social worker nor the client are confident about how to get started, and yet the social worker will take a very authoritative role. The client may be either very self-effacing, or very demanding about what she thinks she needs in order to 'sort herself out'. She may, for example, try to strike a bargain with the social worker, saying that if the worker were to provide a different home-help then she would reduce her drinking. It is vital that the worker and the client work together to find out what short-term goals are appropriate, realistic, and honest. Both the contract that is established and the process of achieving these goals should be genuinely co-operative, based on an accurate assessment of the client's (and the worker's) resources, her needs, and her readiness for personal and behavioural change (see Chapter 3). Social workers must anticipate periods of trial and error, and the likelihood of lapses. They must guard against either colluding with the client, or becoming judgemental or parental.

Alcohol-related problems

There are some problems connected with intoxication, regular, heavy drinking, and alcohol dependence which are unique to women because of their physiology. There are other problems which are more common in women but not exclusive to them, and it is important that these are understood in terms of women's social position and their internalisation of particular values and attitudes. For some female problem drinkers it may take many years to untangle the various threads which have created a web of confusion and destruction. Some of their problems will be located in the structural oppression of women; some may be linked to their physical health; some are to do with their cognitions and self-perception; some are unique to their own emotional make-up.

As has already been stated, in general, women appear to identify a wide range of stressful circumstances and events as causes of their excessive drinking, but they may be less clear that they may be the result of such drinking. In fact, it may be just as useful to regard any 'distress' which either exacerbates or is exacerbated by an individual's drinking patterns as an alcohol-related problem. The task of the social worker is to join with the client in exploring the interaction between the harm or distress, and her pattern and quantity of alcohol consumption.

Physical damage

Intoxication

The short-term effects of alcohol on women's bodies differ from the effects on men in that women become intoxicated quicker and on smaller amounts. How a drinker behaves when intoxicated is to some extent a learned behaviour: for instance an adult man is less likely to become giggly when drunk than an adult woman, but both men and women's capacity to drive safely is impaired when their blood–alcohol level is raised. It is important that public education campaigns draw attention to the fact that a woman's blood–alcohol level rises faster than a man's. Some experiments show that women will reach particularly high-peak blood–alcohol concentrations in the middle of their menstrual cycle, and it also appears that contraceptive pills interfere with the breakdown of alcohol.

Mixing alcohol with other drugs

Approximately 45–65 per cent of Social Services clients seen in area offices or medical settings are taking psychotropic drugs (Rixson and Velleman 1988). The majority of these are women. Regular ongoing use of tranquillisers, sleeping tablets, and anti-depressants can of itself lead to problems (e.g. withdrawal symptoms and self-poisoning) and there are additional dangers when these drugs are taken when there is alcohol in the blood-stream. There is an interaction of the sedating properties of both, so that the functioning of the central nervous system can be drama-tically impaired. There is some evidence that permanent, minimal brain damage can occur, with a resultant reduction in overall cognitive functioning. An overdose of alcohol combined with other

CNS depressant drugs may lead to a deep coma. Also a drinker who has been moderately or severely dependent on alcohol should be particularly careful of relying on other types of drugs as a substitute.

There are a number of other prescribed medications which represent a serious health hazard if combined with alcohol, including several anti-diabetic tablets, anti-coagulants, and anti-epileptic drugs. The drug Flagyl, which is often used to treat vaginal infections, can cause similar effects, when combined with alcohol, to the effects of Antabuse (disulfiram) plus alcohol, namely nausea, flushing, headache, and a fall in blood pressure. An important and little publicised danger is the effect that Antabuse may have on a developing foetus. Psychiatrists, general practitioners, and pregnant women should be alerted to the fact that this deterrent drug has been linked to spontaneous abortion and foetal abnormality (cited in Rossett 1980).

The reproductive system

There is some evidence that continuous heavy drinking may disrupt ovulation, probably as a result of interference with the functioning of the liver and hormone production. Spontaneous abortion may be more likely to occur in those who drink heavily in the first trimester of pregnancy than amongst light drinkers or abstainers. However, research results tend to be contradictory and it has not been possible to agree on a cut-off point below which there is no risk. Recent studies show that links between alcohol and infertility should be investigated in men, as regular heavy drinking has a damaging effect on sperm production and sperm quality. Considerable moral panic and a fair amount of research has been generated in recent years about the effect of maternal alcohol consumption on the foetus. A useful account of current views and a description of a research project in Scotland is provided by Plant (1985) in her book *Women, Drinking and Pregnancy*. The 1986 report of the Royal College of Psychiatrists draws attention to the fact that 'the foetal alcohol syndrome appears to be rare in the United Kingdom and is probably the result of a combination of factors of which alcohol is only one (Royal College of Psychiatrists 1986:100). Some studies show that while heavy maternal drinking is *associated* with birth abnormalities, many other factors – familiar to social workers – are, too, including age, class, diet, obstetric history, smoking, and the use of other drugs, both prescribed and illicit. Emotional stress in pregnant women has also been shown to be a factor in perinatal complications (Rossett 1980), so perhaps social workers and others concerned about the welfare of the newborn should

115

address themselves to the use of alcohol to relieve feelings of chronic depression and anxiety in many heavy-drinking women. Because of the pressure on the social worker to prioritise the needs of the child, and possibly because of an attitude of moral indignation, the social worker may have to try extra hard to concentrate on helping the pregnant client who is drinking heavily. The function that alcohol serves for her, regarding conflict or distress, must be addressed, as well as helping her to find positive alternatives to drinking.

The liver

The severe form of liver damage which can occur and is normally (but not inevitably) associated with chronic heavy drinking is cirrhosis. There are relatively more deaths amongst heavy-drinking women than amongst heavy-drinking men, and a sobering statistic is that whilst the damage may be halted in men by stopping drinking, it may continue to worsen even after a female patient becomes abstinent. This is most likely to occur in women of child-bearing age. There is conflicting evidence about whether women of Afro-Caribbean descent are more prone than white women to cirrhosis; there is some evidence that the disease is increasing more rapidly amongst black women in Britain than amongst white.

Social and emotional damage

Many of the ways in which women's self-worth can be undermined by heavy drinking have been mentioned earlier in this chapter. A downward spiral of self-blame, guilt, helplessness, and increased drinking develops as alcohol problems become more severe. Depression is more readily tolerated in women than 'acting out' behaviour, such as physical or verbal aggression, which is more common in men. It engenders a less punitive response in others, so women may experience greater remorse and guilt than men if their behaviour when drunk affects others. Saunders (in Camberwell Council on Alcohol 1980) points out that excessive drinking 'grossly impairs' the normal sources of self-esteem for most women: their evaluation of their worth tends to be based on social interaction or interpersonal qualities. Deprived of this, the heavy-drinking woman's psychological vulnerability is made worse by society's asssumptions about her inability to function in the traditional female role. She is likely to accept the implied criticisms of those around her – that she is not a capable mother or home-maker, that she is not sexually attractive, that she is literally 'useless'.

It is hardly surprising that women who are alcohol-dependent are seen as being more deviant, more neurotic, or more ill than men. And at a conscious or unconscious level, a woman whose drinking is leading to criticism may find it more functional to display or be treated for more 'feminine' complaints, such as depression, agoraphobia, or anorexia than for their problem drinking. These conditions appear more likely to co-exist with alcohol dependence in women than in men. There is little scientific evidence, however, to indicate whether they normally pre-date the drinking, whether they develop concurrently, or whether they are in some way a response to alcohol dependence having occurred. If the latter is the case, one could speculate that these are socially constructed 'neuroses', used by the helping professions and perhaps by drinkers themselves to lessen the oppressive social and emotional consequences of being 'a women who drinks too much'.

The heavy-drinking man's behaviour is likely to be tolerated by his family and his social acquaintances for a longer period of time than a woman's. A wife is usually in a less powerful position financially and socially than the husband of a female drinker. A woman's drunkenness will more quickly lead to embarrassment and distress amongst her peers than excessive drinking by a man, and she is likely to feel rejected and isolated. She will feel pressure to drink in secret and to attempt to cover up her drinking more than a man, who may well be part of a pub culture or have workmates who are accustomed to his drinking.

There is both psychological and social damage associated with marital breakdown or being ostracised by family members because of drinking. Caring for an elderly female relative at home, for instance, may be regarded by the family as intolerable if the relative seems to be drinking too much. A young woman whose parents regard drinking as a religious or cultural taboo may be rejected completely if she drinks at all. The 'deviant' label is likely then to stick, bringing in its wake confusion, guilt, and social upheaval.

At risk groups

There are some 'categories' of women within which there are more likely to be those who are at risk of developing drink-related problems. Their vulnerability is either because even moderate drinking can cause them harm, or because women in certain groups are not subject to the normal informal 'rules' about drinking, which encourage moderation. This may occur temporarily – for example, when facing a major life crisis – or over an extended period of time.

Adolescent girls may be unaware of their own susceptibility to heavy drinking and there may be strong peer pressure on them to participate in drinking sessions, often with an expectation to 'be sophisticated' and drink spirits. When this occurs over an extended period, some young women may develop a degree of dependence on alcohol. Tolerance to alcohol decreases with age, and in old age the drinker will start to become intoxicated on smaller amounts, so that the likelihood of falls or other accidents increases. Many older women may be taking prescribed medication, and dangerous side-effects often occur when alcohol is mixed with other drugs.

The absence of social controls on the setting, amount, and pattern of a woman's drinking may occur temporarily, or as a consistent theme. A period of solitary heavy drinking is a common, but not well-documented, response to bereavement, the break-up of an important relationship, becoming unemployed, or miscarriage. There is a danger in this becoming too prolonged, as the drinking habit may prevent the woman from developing healthier coping strategies. Some women may be at risk of using alcohol continuously as a way of mitigating unbearable guilt and confusion when she is aware of sexual abuse within her family, or when she is the victim of domestic violence. This may also redirect the focus of any social work intervention away from the source of her underlying distress. Continuous heavy drinking can both mask and exacerbate 'family secrets' and the helper needs to be acutely aware of why the drinker may be fearful of giving it up.

Social isolation is regarded by many to be a major risk factor for women to start drinking heavily. Alcohol is a comparatively cheap and easy way of achieving oblivion, and of filling time. Those whom society marginalises, for instance older, lonely women who are housebound, or those who have psychiatric disabilities, may well become reliant on alcohol. Another group who are at risk are unpaid carers of elderly or disabled relatives, for whom alcohol provides a sense of release and solace. And finally, there is the problem of those who develop harmful drinking habits in response to the drinking habits of their partners.

Women whose partners drink to excess

In most relationships when one partner's drinking is causing overt physical, practical, or emotional problems, the other partner will experience conflict and distress. In heterosexual relationships, a man is very likely to end his relationship if the woman is drinking to excess, whereas women tend to stay with heavy-drinking men for longer. Little is known about patterns of drinking in lesbian relationships, but it is likely that the non-heavy-drinking partner will feel doubly isolated and wary of seeking help, as she may fear judgemental reactions about her sexuality and about the behaviour of her partner. In lesbian and heterosexual relationships there are loyalties, conflicts, and emotional dependencies which the outsider may find difficult to understand. The partner may go to extremes to protect and defend the drinker, putting up with apparently intolerable behaviour towards her. She may find it difficult to admit that there is anything unusual or hurtful about her partner's drinking patterns, of if she does, she often sees herself as being to blame for it.

A wish to cover up or minimise the partner's drinking, and the acceptance of some or total responsibility for it, needs to be acknowledged and worked through if the social worker is to gain the trust of the woman client in this situation. Moral indignation or disbelief at the woman's loyalty will prevent the practitioner from understanding what may be a long-established pattern, where the possibility of change is more frightening than the status quo. The dynamics within the relationship may be similar to those in which a woman is the victim of domestic violence, or where she suspects that her partner is abusing her children.

The woman client needs to be given 'permission' to talk about the role alcohol plays in her personal and family relationships. She needs to be given clear and honest information about whether what she talks about will be passed on to anyone else. She needs to be shown that the worker is 'on her side' and will work with her at her own pace. She will need to unload her fears, anger, and feelings of loyalty, confusion, and self-blame. Confrontation between the woman and her partner often follows such an unloading, sometimes resulting in the partner storming out and leaving the woman more vulnerable, or alternatively, in a tearful show-down in which sincere promises of a change in behaviour are made. The social worker should be prepared for the repercussions: the woman may feel that she was in the wrong either way, and she may regret having brought up the subject with her partner, and having spoken to anyone else about his behaviour. She needs to be helped to accept that she has made a start, and that she is entitled to time and 'space' and help from others to identify what she wants from the relationship and how she can best negotiate this. Within an empathic relationship, social workers can offer considerable emotional and practical help to clients who are in this situation. They should also be aware of publications such as *Families and Alcoholics* by Alison Burr (1982), the help provided by the self-help network, Al-Anon, and the availability of help at local Councils on Alcohol.

Policy and practice

In social work, as in the medical profession, policy-making is dominated by men: there are few women in senior management positions, and budgets are primarily controlled by men. Given the judgemental attitudes of society to women who drink too much, female clients with alcohol-related problems are particularly vulnerable to social work policy and practice discounting their needs, in favour of short-term crisis management, and dealing with the real or imagined effects of their drinking on others. To make matters worse, many Social Services and Social Work Departments are overstretched and under-resourced, and they may actively discourage individual practitioners from working on long-term behaviour change with their clients. This makes it particularly important that in working with women who have drinking problems, the practitioner is aware of the ambivalence, confused attitudes, and uncertainty about the nature of alcohol problems, and that she defines very clearly what it is honest and realistic for her to undertake. Broadly speaking, the worker should clarify which of the following areas will be the main focus of attention: (1) managing crisis; (2) reducing long-term harm to the drinker or her family; or (3) techniques to help the drinker change her behaviour.

The types of intervention required will be very different, although the practitioner may work with the same individual client in these three areas at different times. Referring to the terminology used in this book, managing a crisis applies mainly to dealing with serious or recurring episodes of intoxication, harm-reduction is most applicable when regular, heavy drinking is the main concern, and various techniques may be relevant when alcohol dependence is the central problem. Also, constructive approaches to altering drinking behaviour or stopping altogether can only occur once the contemplation stage has been worked through (see Chapters 3 and 6) and the client is at the action stage. The practitioner will also need to ensure that the help continues through the maintenance and the relapse-prevention stage.

In focusing on different interventions at different periods in the drinker's life, the practitioner needs to be aware that crisis management *may* be viewed by the client as 'rescuing', and harm-reduction (especially for the family) *may* be seen as persecutory. Thus, for example, the social worker may at first try to remove some of the pressures on a woman whose drinking is out of hand (for instance, if she is about to be evicted), and help her through a critical time. Then if there were, say, serious problems with her child truanting from school and stealing, and there is an attempt to reduce long-term harm in the family by having the child fostered, the social worker is in the position of exerting power over the drinker, and may be seen as the persecutor. As there is strong pressure within the social-work role to perform these sorts of tasks, it is not easy for the individual practitioner to then step into the therapeutic role, which the drinker will need if she is to make real changes in her drinking behaviour. She needs to accept responsibility for the consequences of her drinking, but yet the social worker is required to protect those around her from the harmful effects of a problem drinker. Social workers should attempt at all times to be honest with the client, and with their own line-manager and agency, so that major role conflicts can be avoided whenever possible.

In practice, effective interventions with women problem drinkers will also depend on the role and setting within which the practitioner works. Where the social worker has a large caseload or many statutory responsibilities, there will be less opportunity for working for direct behavioural change, and the worker will need to concentrate on managing crises or minimising potential harm to the drinker and her family. If she is ready to seek change for herself, the drinker can be helped to find a self-help group, counselling agency, or other treatment facility, bearing in mind the kinds of barriers which may get in the way. Where the practitioner's role is to work with certain vulnerable client groups, such as older women, or women who are on tranquillisers or other drugs, who may be reluctant to acknowledge the existence of a drink problem, it is *their* responsibility to introduce the topic of drinking: a starting point for intervention should be to highlight why drink is appealing and why it can be dangerous, in an informative and non-judgemental way. For example, the practitioner may say: 'Many people in situations similar to yours may find themselves gradually drinking more than they used to – it's a useful way of coping, at first. Do you find that your drinking habits have changed at all?' In some settings, it may be possible and appropriate for the social worker to set up discussion groups, for instance, in residential and day-care settings.

Social workers can be a powerful force of change in a woman drinker's life – they are likely to have more of an overview of her situation and be in touch with her for a longer period of time than many other 'helping professionals'. Working effectively with the female drinker can be immensely rewarding to both worker and client. Whatever the setting, and whatever pressures they are under, social workers need to start by trying to understand the ways in which their views of women and drinking may influence their intervention. The embarrassment and guilt which we all carry, which reinforces clients' reluctance to regard alcohol-related problems as legitimate areas to be helped with, need to be faced. First and foremost, questions about drinking patterns should be included in the normal intake interviews and in the social enquiry reports which all social workers undertake. Information about the consequences of heavy drinking, and the characteristics of alcohol dependence, must be brought up in individual discussions and groupwork, with particular reference to the situation of most women. The link between 'presenting problems' and drinking habits should be made openly by a social worker and client together, not through the social worker secretly trying to piece together clues and suspicions, and using them in evidence against the client. When the social workers says: 'You need help', the woman client needs to know if that really means that the worker is 'on her side'. At all times, social workers need to remain sensitive to the shame and fears of the woman who drinks to excess, and at the same time they should seek to challenge the moralistic and inaccurate perceptions of society and many of its 'helping institutions'.

© 1990 Rosemary Kent

References

Avon Council on Alcohol (1982) *Women and Alcohol: a survey of gateways to treatment for women in Avon*, Bristol: Avon Council on Alcohol.

Breeze, E. (1985) *Women and Drinking*, an enquiry carried out on behalf of the DHSS, London: HMSO.

Brook, E. and Davis, A. (eds) (1985) *Women, The Family and Social Work*, London: Tavistock.

Broverman, I.K., Broverman, D., Clarkson, F., Rosenkrantz, P., and Vogel, S. (1970) 'Sex role stereotypes and clinical judgements of mental health', *Journal of Consulting and Clinical Psychology*, 34:1–7.

Burr, A. (1982) *Families and Alcoholics*, London: Constable.

Burtle, V. (ed.) (1979) *Women Who Drink: alcoholic experience and psychotherapy*, Illinois: Thomas Springfield.

Camberwell Council on Alcoholism (eds) (1980) *Women and Alcohol*, London: Tavistock.

Cook, D.J. and Allan, C.A. (1984) 'Stressful life events and alcohol abuse in women: a general population study', *British Journal of Addiction* 79:425–30.

DAWN (Drugs Alcohol Women Nationally) (1985) *Survey of Facilities for Women Using Drugs (Including Alcohol) in London*, London: DAWN.

Evans, M. and Ungerson, C. (eds) (1983) *Sexual Divisions: patterns and processes*, London: Tavistock.

Goddard, E. and Ikin, C. (1988) *Drinking in England and Wales in 1987*, OPCS Social Surveys Division, SS1283, London: HMSO.

Hunt, L. (1982) *Alcohol Related Problems*, London: Heinemann Educational Books.

Hutter, N. and Williams, G. (1981) *Controlling Women: the normal and the deviant*, London: Croom Helm.

Isaacs, J. and Moon, G. (1985) *Alcohol Problems: the social work response*, SSRIU Report no. 13, Portsmouth Polytechnic.

Kalant, O.J. (ed.) (1980) *Alcohol and Drug Problems in Women*, New York: Plenum Press.

Keil, T.J. (1978) 'Sex role variations and women's drinking', *Journal of Studies on Alcohol* 39:859–68.

Kent, R. (1989) *Say When: everything a woman needs to know about alcohol and drinking problems*, London: Sheldon Press.

McConville, B. (1983) *Women under the Influence*, London: Virago Press.

MacLennan, A. (ed.) (1976) *Women: their use of alcohol and other legal drugs*, Toronto, Canada: Addiction Research Foundation.

Mayer, J. and Black, R. (1977) 'The relationship between alcoholism and child abuse and neglect' in F.A. Seixas (ed.) *Currents in Alcoholism*, vol. 2, New York: Grune and Stratton.

Mintel (1987) *Changing Lifestyles in the Alcoholic Drinks Market*, cited in J. Robinson *On the Demon Drink*, London: Mitchell Beazley.

Orford, J. (1975) 'Alcoholism and marriage: the argument against specialism', *Journal of Studies on Alcohol* 36(11):1537–63.

Plant, M. (1985) *Women, Drinking and Pregnancy*, London: Tavistock.

Rixson, A. and Velleman, R. (1988) 'Prescribing alternatives to psychotropic drugs', *Social Work Today* 20(15):13–15.

Robinson, J. (1988) *On the Demon Drink*, London: Mitchell Beazley.

Rossett, H.L. (1980) 'The effects of alcohol on the foetus and offspring', in O.J. Kalant (ed.) *Alcohol and Drug Problems in Women*, New York: Plenum Press.

Royal College of Psychiatrists (1986) *Alcohol: our favourite drug*, London: Tavistock.

Sandmaier, M. (1980) *The Invisible Alcoholics – Women and Alcohol Abuse in America*, New York: McGraw-Hill.

Saunders, B. (1980) 'Psychological aspects of women and alcohol' in Camberwell Council on Alcoholism (eds) *Women and Alcohol*, London: Tavistock.

Steiner, C. (1979) *Healing Alcoholism*, New York: Grove Press.

Shaw, S., Cartwright, A., Spratley, T., and Harwin, J. (1978) *Responding to Drinking Problems*, London: Croom Helm.

Sheehan, M. and Watson, J. (1980) 'Response and recognition' in Camberwell Council on Alcoholism (eds) *Women and Alcohol*, London: Tavistock.

Social Work Services Group (1987) *Practice Guidance – Towards Effective Practice with Problem Drinkers*, Edinburgh: Social Work Services Group.

Shaw, S. (1980) 'The causes of increasing drinking problems amongst women – a general etiological theory', in Camberwell Council on Alcoholism (eds) *Women and Alcohol*, London: Tavistock.

Thom, B. (1986) 'Sex differences in help-seeking for alcohol problems', *British Journal of Addiction* 81:777–8.

Waterson, J., Ettore, B., Griffiths, R., and Kent, R. (eds) (1986) 'Women's Problems with alcohol and other drugs – improving our response', proceedings of a conference held in July. University of Kent, Canterbury: Alcohol Interventions Training Unit.

Wilsnack, S.C. (1976) 'The impact of sex roles on women's alcohol use and abuse', in M. Greenblatt and M.A. Schuckit (eds) *Alcoholism Problems in Women and Children*, New York: Grune and Stratton.

Wilsnack, S.C. and Beckman, L.J. (eds) (1984) *Alcohol Problems in Women*, New York: Guilford Press.

Wolfson, D. and Murray, J. (eds) (1986) *Women and Dependency*, London: DAWN.

Chapter five

Helping the family

Graham Fanti

Human beings are by nature social creatures. From birth onwards, we are maintained in a framework of intimate human connections. A vital part of this framework is the family and yet, as an influential and needy group in itself, it is offered few helping services. In reality an alcohol problem rarely remains an individual's sole property. Invariably where a problem drinker is a member of a family, he or she creates harm for those others close to them. So how can the family's resources be best utilised to help the one doing the harmful drinking and, perhaps more importantly, to help themselves? This chapter will address these questions.

The family connection

As a unit, the family is complex and subject to almost continual change. Skynner (1976) poetically describes it as the 'interface where youth meets age, and birth and death are juxtaposed, linking the inner with the outer world, the individual with the group'. Thus helping strategies must account for the special nature of families.

Family members experiencing alcohol problems will display differences in behaviour and affect at certain times. Their family will notice these alterations. On seeing these changes, they may offer to help resolve the individual's problems or, should they be threatening the stability of the family, may demand certain actions of the problem maker. Should these changes not take place, the family members have to decide how to continue to meet their own and the family's needs in the light of this new problem. Ways of adjusting around the problem may be sought in order to keep the family intact or the family may, as a last resort, ask the problem drinker to leave the unit. As a rule, families will often attempt to absorb problems in order to continue functioning as a whole. This tendency to maintain stability is termed homeostasis.

Minuchin (1981) describes the family as a living system which interacts with its internal and external environment. Any fluctuation in the family system is usually followed by a reaction that is intended to stabilise the system once more. A major change can induce a family crisis, which in turn transforms the family, causing it to develop a new level of functioning. The major change is thus absorbed, leading to a stable state based on an adapted way of interacting.

A repeated difficulty, such as alcohol-related poverty, does not necessarily present the family with the same depth of problem as on the first occasion it was encountered. With time, the family may come to expect the problem to occur on a regular basis and develop strategies to adjust their functioning to counter the resultant problems. Alcohol-related difficulties can be absorbed by families, becoming an accepted part of family living. The increasing severity of the difficulty and the wider the range of problems presenting, can lead to a family taking on an increasingly alcohol-focused lifestyle themselves. Indeed, the problematic use of alcohol may bring with it some benefits to the family itself, which is valued over and above the negative consequences.

Steinglass (1976) labelled such a situation as the 'Alcoholic System' in which the 'presence or absence of alcohol becomes the single most important variable' determining the family's interaction. Alcohol use can assume a central position in the life of families, becoming a major organising factor in family life.

The vital role that the presence and absence of alcohol has on couple interaction was noted in the observations of jointly admitted couples to an in-patient Alcohol Treatment Unit (Steinglass 1977). Here the couples were encouraged to live normally with continued alcohol consumption and later without any alcohol use. The resultant range of interaction between intoxicated couples was narrowed in terms of affect and physical behaviour compared to that seen when they were 'dry'. Within this narrowed range the 'wet' behaviour took on a more automated quality (Steinglass 1979). Implicit in these observations is the belief that drinking enables the couple to either avoid certain issues, or deal with others not covered whilst in a 'dry' state.

Families with alcohol problems which were two years post-treatment were compared by Moos *et al.* (1984) with matched families with no history of alcohol problems. The results showed that those families which had resolved their alcohol problems functioned similarly to those without previous alcohol problems. Families with alcohol problems following relapse were different in that they had less family cohesion, expression, reaction, and agreement about problems. As well as this, the role functions, of family members were affected, i.e. the non-drinking parent tended to do more household tasks and the problem-drinking parent less. Work by Vannicelli *et al.* (1983) supports this, indicating that families adjusting to sobriety experience stress as a consequence but they are by and large not disrupted. Families resolving their own drinking problems tend to experience more negative affect than those not succeeding in their problem resolution.

Alcohol-related difficulties can occur at any stage in the family's development. It may be at the very beginning, where a family member, usually a partner, already has a problem with alcohol, or at the end, where a grandparent encounters problems in old age. Clearly, different family members may develop an alcohol problem at different stages of their life. There may even be more than one person whose drinking is causing alcohol problems at any one time.

The repeated use of alcohol by an individual family member, despite resultant problems, should be seen as not only negative in effect. The use has a positive effect that the user values over and above the cost of the resulting damage. This balancing act fluctuates with time. There will be the occasions when the consumer feels that their alcohol use is causing difficulties which far outweigh the benefits of use. It is at these crisis points that the user is susceptible to major functional change.

Familial alcohol problems

The kinds of alcohol-related problems that can be experienced within any one family can vary considerably. Two families with exactly the same structure, say a single father with two teenage boys, may have very different problems, even though both fathers drink the same quantities with the same frequency. There are many factors that influence which problems families may experience. Any of the following factors can apply; such as individual personality, the strength of family relationships, the family rules, individual perceptions, family wealth, frequency of drinking, local status, community integration, and the laws of the land.

The problems can be broken down into 3 main areas: physical, psychological, and social. No family is exactly the same but there can be similarities. What follows is a breakdown of the kinds of difficulties that can occur in the family as a whole and to the different members that may live within the family unit.

The family as a whole

Physically

The family may experience alcohol-related poverty leading to nutritional neglect, insufficient fuel, clothing, and poor housing conditions. Holidays may become rare and other whole family treats, such as eating out together and day trips, may be similarly infrequent or absent.

Psychologically

The psychological effects on the alcohol-focused family are clearly described by Wegscheider (1981) in her consideration of family roles. She suggests that each family member takes on a specific family role in an attempt to counterbalance the difficulties brought on by problem drinking. These roles enable the family to function despite its alcohol focus, keeping together a system that would otherwise fall apart. The roles described by Wegscheider are as follows:

The enabler   The family member who is emotionally closest to the problem drinker usually takes on the role of 'the enabler'. Their role is to support the alcohol misuser, allowing them to function as freely as possible whilst avoiding their drinking consequences. The enabler delays the crises that may threaten the problem drinker, which in turn threaten the family stability. He or she regularly covers for the drinker's behaviour and takes over the responsibility for maintaining the family.

Where the problem drinker is a parent, the enabler is usually the spouse. The enabler is most likely to be the eldest child where the problem drinker is a single parent. If the alcohol misuser is the eldest child, then one or more of the parents are liable to fulfil the enabling role.

The enabler tends to adjust his or her own actions so as to counterbalance the actions of the family's problem drinker. A regular cycle of persecutor, rescuer, and victim roles are played out by both participants in the game termed the Karpman Triangle (Steiner 1971). The victim acts helpless and ashamed, the rescuer wants to help the poor victim, and the persecutor feels angry, particularly when the rescuing fails. The roles are swopped and intended to complement each other and never coincide; the goal is to dampen down the drinking effects on the family, thus preventing family breakdown. But family members are not always the only players. The social worker trying to help the problem drinker can also become a participant, stepping in for an absent enabler. This kind of involvement can be very destructive to the social work task and social workers and their supervisors should be constantly watching out for its presence.

The hero   The oasis in the desert, 'the hero' is an important addition to the problem drinker and the enabler. The hero is the distraction from reality of chaotic family life. This role is to be the figurehead of the family in terms of achievement. The hero is the symbol on to which the family pins its fantasy that everything at home is OK. Consequently, he or she cannot show how sad they really feel. Isolated, they gain attention by doing better each time, pushing themselves further to gain rare praise, and in the process, to rescue the family from the belief that all is not well. The hero tends to have low self-esteem, feeling guilty and inadequate as he or she is unable to reach the distant targets he or she constantly sets. Typically, the hero is the eldest child of a family with one or more parents with drinking problems.

The scapegoat   Outside of the triad of problem drinker, enabler, and hero, 'the scapegoat' can only attract attention through troublesome behaviour. Always defiant and anti-social, the scapegoat is the clothes hook to hang the family's troubles on. At times of impending family crisis, the scapegoat acts to distract the family from the possible problem, rescuing the family by attracting attention to his or her own behaviour. The scapegoat is openly blamed for all the family's troubles – the 'black sheep' of the family.

The lost child   Like the scapegoat, 'the lost child' fails to secure regular family attention and through unassertive behaviour, unlike the scapegoat, causes no difficulties. Almost invisible to the other family members, the lost child is isolated, unadventurous, and has poor self-worth.

The mascot   'The mascot' has much in common with the scapegoat and lost child. The triad of problem drinker, enabler, and hero is out of their reach and the fleeting snatches of attention are gained through exaggerated behaviour. In this case, the mascot is the family joker, providing the light relief in a stressful environment. Often inappropriate in action, the mascot compulsively fights for attention through humour, which disguises his or her own real sense of fear.

Socially

The family as a whole may experience gradual social isolation from relatives and friends. Any new family friends are more likely to have a similar alcohol-focused life themselves. In families with serious hardship, statutory agencies such as the police, Probation Services, Education Welfare and Social Services may become involved in helping the family to resolve short-term crises and to place boundaries on family behaviour where these have not been internally set.

The partners

Physically

Alcohol-related family violence is often focused on the partner of the problem drinker. Orford *et al.* (1976) studied the wives of 100 husbands undergoing treatment for alcoholism at a London clinic and found that nearly half of the wives had been beaten and just over one in four had experienced attempts to severely injure them. Gayford (1975) examined 100 cases of wives who had experienced violence from their partners. Just over half of the violent partners were frequently drunk in the domiciliary home and another fifth had episodes of heavy drinking. Another study showed alcohol and family violence to be closely related, with violence being 'twice as likely to occur in families with rather than without alcohol problems' (Byles 1978).

Psychologically

The problem drinker's preoccupation with alcohol-focused activities can lead to the partner taking on full organisational responsibility for the family. In effect, the partner begins to function as a one-parent family, with an additional dependant – their problem-drinking partner. The responsibility entailed in not only dealing single-handedly with everyday family affairs but also coping with alcohol problems, can lead to considerable emotional strains for the partner. There becomes less time to relax and take care of his or her own needs. As problems deteriorate and become crises the partner may blame him/herself for not coping, experiencing anxiety and depressive states, instead of looking to the drinking partner to help the family.

Sexual difficulties may be present in the relationship, resulting from the emotional pressures on one or both partners or the physiological effect of alcohol use on the problem-drinking partner (Wilson 1984).

Socially

The partner may suffer increasing social isolation as a consequence of his or her partner's drinking behaviour. Friends that pre-date the relationship may be lost and new friends may be more interested in the couple's drinking lifestyle than other aspects. The problem drinker may jealously choose to make it difficult for his or her spouse to meet and make new friends, with the intention of controlling the spouse's life. The more control the drinking partner has, the less opportunity the spouse has to leave.

Parents

Physically

Parents may be subjected to violence or accidents during attempts to deal with their intoxicated offspring. Age can be an influence in this respect, in that an elderly parent may no longer be able to cope with the exertion involved and be more vulnerable to physical attack. Where the parents are totally dependent on their problem-drinking adult children, they may experience neglect in terms of inadequate food, heating, and other basic necessities through a resulting lack of adequate income.

Psychologically

Low self-esteem, guilt, and feeling responsible for the family's problems may cause a parent to experience anxiety and phobic and depressive states. These can lead to the inappropriate prescription of anti-depressants and minor tranquillisers and in the more extreme cases, admissions to psychiatric hospitals.

Socially

Parents living with their problem-drinking offspring may become isolated from the rest of their family and friends, as others choose to avoid the drinking problem. They may experience an increasing narrowing of their social lives, becoming more reliant on the problem drinker and thus less likely to break away, as their lives increasingly cease to provide opportunities to escape the problem.

Children

Physically

Child abuse, including sexual abuse, and neglect constitute the most serious harm to children. Alcohol misuse is one of the most commonly cited factors in the family backgrounds of such cases. An NSPCC analysis of a five-year period of referrals to their child-abuse registers found one in five to have alcohol use as a stress factor (Creighton 1984). A study of 250 Social Services Department family cases in Bristol (Abel 1983) indicated one in five to have alcohol problems. Nearly one-third of those families with alcohol problems were on the Department's 'At Risk' Register. A recent study by Devon County Council (Mather 1988) found that just over a quarter of registered child abuse cases and a third of children in care were from families with drinking problems.

Psychologically

Tension, conflict, inconsistency, and role confusion can be daily occurrences which affect the psychological well-being of children who live in families where there are drinking problems. They may avoid going home after school as they are afraid as to what awaits them on their return. Conversely, they may be scared to go to school for fear of a parent harming themselves in their absence. Broken promises can lead to strained family relationships and a lack of trust. The child may develop anxiety, phobic and depressive states, and in some cases, the child may attempt self-harm (Seixas 1979).

An area receiving little attention is the needs of adults who grew up in families with alcohol problems. The USA has seen new initiatives in this field in recent years. Black has specialised in this work and she suggests that common problems in later life are a result of growing up in chaotic family environments. Examples of some of the common problems are learning not to cry or crying alone, over-whelming fear, unresolved guilt, and anger. The inability to trust can be a problem and the need to control situations may be a product. Black considers one of the biggest single problems for the adult children of problem-drinking families is the inability to ask others to help them (Black 1981).

Socially

Social lives of children can be severely restricted if members of their family have alcohol problems. They may be too embarrassed to bring their friends home for fear of a scene or purely because they do not want their friends to see the state of their house if it is being neglected. In these situations it is easier not to bring the friend home at all.

The family model

One of the major difficulties for social workers dealing with alcohol problems is knowing how to put the immediate difficulty into context. Is the presenting problem new to the family? How threatening is it to their stability? Is the problem a repeated part of a chaotic alcohol-focused lifestyle? How and when should the social workers respond in a way that helps the family eliminate its focus upon alcohol?

The model outlined in this section suggests a practical understanding of how families function in systems where substance abuse problems exist – in this case alcohol. The use of this model will enable social workers to identify the present stage in which the family is functioning. It is an extension of Steinglass's earlier work on the life history of alcohol problems in families (Steinglass 1980).

Families essentially function in one of three states, the 'three Cs' – calm, chaos, and crisis. Calm is where no particular difficulty is occurring for the family. Chaos is where the system is under stress but not threatened, particularly if the family has experience of resolving such a difficulty. Crisis is the family state resulting from a new problem which endangers the entire stability of the family. The ability to identify the presenting state is vital to being able to help families with their alcohol problems. A family in a state of calm may not be receptive to major structural change in their lifestyle. Neither will a family going through a chaotic state, although they will be interested in any help a social worker can offer to reduce the immediate effects of their present alcohol difficulty. But a family experiencing a crisis will be interested in major structural change because they believe, at this point, that things can never return to how they were.

Understandably, families will present to social workers for help, when there is either chaotic functioning or a crisis occurring. The key is ensuring that the structural change occurs in such a way as to eliminate the problem alcohol use and not just the presenting problem alone. Chaotic states will inevitably be more frequent than crises, consequently social workers should be wary of too readily resolving chaotic alcohol-related events. Temporarily ending financial problems for instance, can often delay the appearance of crises that provoke change.

The social worker also needs to be careful that his or her actions do not lead to their taking on the role of family enabler themselves, joining in the Karpman triangle of rescuer, persecutor, and victim on a regular basis. The trap is often apparent when the social worker displays a lack of energy and confidence, having been emotionally exhausted by the family. Unable to keep his or her objectivity, the social worker may enter a repetitive cycle of saving the family, and thus the problem drinker, from a chaotic situation, then later berating the problem drinker for unhelpful behaviour and finally feeling ineffectual and guilty for not preventing the next related problem. A social worker trapped in the enabling role may find him/herself undertaking tasks alien to alcohol specialists such as buying alcohol for clients in order to try to control the clients' intake – a classic example amongst home helps, regularly counselling an intoxicated client – or finally, frequently tidying up after, or indeed even putting to bed, a drunk and incapable client.

The danger is that the social worker, and consequently their agency and its scarce resources, may become a regular part of the family's problem-drinking pattern. The catch is the social worker's belief that he or she alone can protect the family from severe disruption. Thus, through this process he or she may prevent the family from experiencing an alcohol-related crisis. Steiner (1974) wisely compares resolving the presenting chaotic problem and not addressing the alcohol cause as equivalent to carrying out 'plastic surgery on a terminal patient'. Not addressing the alcohol issue means that most helping actions are doomed to long-term failure.

Families usually seek stability. Where possible, their major goal is to maintain the family unit and this is achieved by absorbing threatening changes. These attempts to absorb may involve considerable personal sacrifices on the part of some family members. A crisis destabilises the system and leaves it open to new ways of functioning. If the crisis is not a natural life difficulty, such as the birth of a first child or death of a family member, but directly relates to problematic alcohol use, then the crisis is an opportunity for alcohol change. Family members will not be interested in dealing with alcohol issues if the presenting crisis is not directly linked to alcohol use in the family.

A crisis is the resultant upset in a steady state caused by a stress for which the system does not have a coping response. The stress is such that those in the system believe that there must be major change as they can no longer function as before. Thus a crisis related to alcohol use can be a major opportunity for familial change. It represents both danger and opportunity. Time limits crises – few last more than a week in most people's lives. Hence it is important to be able to recognise the arrival of a crisis state, as opposed to a chaotic state, if the worker is to utilise its strength. In addition, the crisis brings back into play unresolved issues from the past, which may add to the depth of the crisis. Thus an alcohol-related crisis can bring into prominence previous drinking difficulties, which in turn, strengthen the argument for change in alcohol use (Parad *et al.* 1965; O'Hagan 1986). Of course, most social workers will be familiar with crisis intervention from their training courses and previous experiences.

Social workers will be conscious that there are statutory responsibilities, particularly with regard to children, that may lead to their own intervention into the family. The introduction of legal action to protect family members experiencing alcohol-related harm can create a family crisis. Jenkins (1989) suggests that a worker may seek to use such a crisis to provoke change, especially in long-term cases where little change is taking place. Any contemplation of crisis induction should bear in mind, though, the differing abilities to cope within the alcohol-focused family. Where possible, the social worker should seek to ensure that no other member is put at serious risk as a result of any protective intervention.

No individual is an 'island' and neither is the family. Family life can be considered as internally and externally interactive. As a part of the environment within which families function, social workers can be in a position of influence. The family model I am proposing breaks down alcohol-focused family functioning into various levels of stable and unstable problem drinking and non-problem drinking. The framework functions on seven levels which are now described.

Level 1. Stable problem-drinking behaviour

The vast majority of problem-drinking family behaviour occurs on level 1. A cycle of states occur within which problematic drinking is contained by one or more family members. Here the family alternates between calm and chaotic behaviour. The calm state is disrupted by a stress related to alcohol, which leads to a chaotic state, following which the family brings into play coping skills developed previously. These skills in turn dampen the effect of the stress, enabling the necessary adjustment to occur which takes the family to its original calm state. The cycle is repeated again and again. It represents a stable level within which the family functions and during this time one or more members continues to drink problematically.

Most alcohol-related cases will present to social workers at this level or at the next level, when the family is in crisis, and by definition, open to change.

Level 2. Alcohol-related crisis states

A stress for which the family has no learned coping response leads the family from chaos into a crisis state. At the crisis stage there can also be an adjustment which returns the family to the calm state of level 1. However, this crisis state can, in turn, lead on to unstable problem-drinking behaviour.

Level 3. Unstable problem-drinking behaviour

The intervening alcohol crisis can move the system onto level 3 where the system ends its stable characteristics. This is a temporary situation and threatening to the previously stable manner of functioning within the family. It represents a crucial opportunity for positive change and, like all crisis states, will be short-lived. From this level, there are 3 options. Either:

(a) a return through adjustment onto the stable cycle of level 1; or
(b) the splitting up of the family via divorce or separation; or
(c) the progression into the transitional level 4.

Level 4. Transitional states

This level represents the positive, productive intervention of the crisis state into the previous, problematic drinking pattern. The members of the family continue to live together and the unstable family behaviour remains but there is a change in that actual problem drinking ends and the unstable family state moves from 'wet' to 'dry'.

Level 5. Harm-free drinking/abstinence

The unstable drinking behaviour continues, even though the family is now functioning with harm-free drinking or abstinence. As before, one of the possibilities includes members leaving the family.

Level 6. Dry, stable, problem-drinking *behaviour*

On achieving this level the family have progressed to a stable state but no problem drinking actually takes place. Relationships and roles within the family remain essentially the same but the frequency of chaotic states will decline as there are no problem-drinking stresses to spark such states off. The system functions are still based on problem drinking and there may be family disagreements occurring *as if* problem drinking had occurred despite its absence. This stable state can continue for long periods, unless a relapse back to problematic drinking takes place.

The term 'dry drunk' is used to describe individuals who have stopped drinking but still carry out the same lifestyle. This term may similarly be used to describe the family functioning at this level. Many members of Alcoholics Anonymous function on level 6 in the belief they cannot attain level 7, and, in some cases, they stay at this level for life.

Level 7. Dry, stable, non-problem drinking behaviour

This is the most secure of the family levels. It is, in essence, the same level as other families in the community who do not have members with drinking problems. Problem-drinking families achieve this level through hard work, flexibility, and time. For some, it can take years to reach this level. En route, the family may have to develop new skills and rediscover personalities and relationships lost in their family's history. Their attainment of this level does not mean that all will now be secure for the family. Natural life difficulties will present, unrelated to drinking (such as bereavement, job loss, and divorce), which act as crises and may lead the family back to previous alcohol-related ways of functioning as a means of trying to cope. In addition, it may be that the previously problematic drinker, or indeed drinkers in some instances, may decide they are dissatisfied with their new lifestyle and attempt to return to problem drinking.

The attainment of this level is most often sought by agencies providing services for drinking problems, although level 6 is often accepted as second best.

The framework

The aim of the framework, and its seven levels, is to enable the social worker to understand the history of the family's alcohol problem as well as their present situation. There are three stable family states: wet, stable, problem drinking behaviour; dry, stable, problem drinking behaviour; and dry, stable, non-problem drinking behaviour. The family will exist in one of these three stable states for the majority of their family life together.

Probably the most common state within which the families will present to social workers is predictably that of wet, stable, problem drinking when they will be in a chaotic or, less commonly, a crisis situation. The goal of all social work action should be to move the family on to the dry, stable state, where functioning is not based on a problematic alcohol use.

The case example which follows demonstrates how the framework can be applied to social work practice. The Jones family's life together is followed over a 9-year period and their actions on their alcohol-related problems are considered.

A case example – the Jones family

Stephen Jones lives with his partner, Helen, on a small, modern estate on the outskirts of Tayor, South Wales. He works as a foreman in a local foundry and Helen, a laboratory assistant, is having a break in her career to look after their new baby, Trevor, aged 2 months.

Stephen has been drinking excessively for seven years following on from his days as a prop forward in the Tayor Town rugby team. They met at a club dance and Helen has always known him to drink heavily. Since the arrival of their baby, Helen has had to change her lifestyle to cope. She no longer goes out late to parties and she has to get up at all hours of the night to care for the needs of their new arrival. Stephen, on the other hand, has not changed his lifestyle. He continues going out to the pub most nights and when at home he happily consumes his alcohol via cans of extra strong beer in front of the TV. Helen has taken on all the responsibility of caring for the baby; Stephen has not. Their income has reduced through Helen no longer working, but their expenditure remains the same. The family is under alcohol-related stress.

Five months later, Helen becomes ill and is admitted to hospital. This creates a family crisis, as she is too ill to have Trevor with her. Fortunately, Stephen's mother helps out during the day and Stephen has to stay at home in the evenings to look after Trevor. This puts the drinking activities of Stephen in conflict with his care of Trevor. He drinks at home as before, and finds himself resenting Trevor for preventing him enjoying his usual activities down the pub. One evening after drinking heavily, Stephen drops Trevor, causing an arm fracture. The continued crying of the baby leads to Stephen contacting his mother for help. She, in turn, takes the child to the local casualty department. The junior doctor on call notes that Stephen smells strongly of alcohol and alerts the Social Services Department 'Out of Hours' team to investigate the injury further.

The resulting social work contact creates an alcohol-related stress which sends the family system into crisis. In this instance, everyone recognises the role of alcohol in the injury to Trevor. The child is placed on the 'At Risk' Register and a social worker is allocated. Helen is furious with Stephen and their marriage is placed in jeopardy, as Helen clearly chooses the needs of their baby in preference to Stephen's alcohol needs. Stephen accepts that his alcohol-related behaviour was the cause of the problem and undertakes to deal with his drinking.

Stephen stops drinking for four weeks after substituting low-alcohol drinks. He still continues his lifestyle as before, going to the pub, etc. and his mother moves in to care fully for Trevor in Helen's absence. This arrangement has the agreement of the local Social Services Department as Stephen's mother guarantees the safety of the baby. Helen's return from hospital allows mother to be less involved, although she continues to support by babysitting for the couple. Stephen's free time is still spent in alcohol-focused settings. He returns to drinking alcohol with Helen's blessing, as she finds his discontentment difficult to handle while dry. She agrees to his drinking on his promise that it will be lower than before and create no problems. This new arrangement is also accepted by the Social Services Department, as the care of Trevor is secured via Helen and her mother, who have promised that Trevor will never be left alone with Stephen following drinking.

Unfortunately, the couple return to their same, previous pattern of functioning. Stephen recommences his old pattern of drinking and Helen adjusts her role, with the support of mother, to meet the needs of the Social Services Department. Thus, Stephen has made no long-term adjustment, although he did have a temporary dry period of four weeks and the crisis is over. The family system has adjusted only slightly in response to the alcohol-related crisis. It has managed to maintain the homeostasis and the central role of alcohol within the system. The intervention of the Social Services Department has been taken into account and dealt with in such a way as to enable the drinking-focused lifestyle of the family to continue.

Two years on, another child, Emma, is born. Mother again takes over the care of the family while Helen has Emma in hospital. The inclusion of Emma in the family membership constitutes a family stress but not a crisis. Helen expects to take on the extra responsibilities involved in her care, as was the case with Trevor. Although she regularly complains about her situation to Stephen at times of disagreement, she never expects change and neither does Stephen. The family now have few friends who are not involved in social activities based on heavy drinking. Those that do not have the same drink-focused activities are seen as boring by Stephen. Helen has few friends and her life has become very heavily focused on the needs of Trevor, Emma, and Stephen. Her mother-in-law, though, continues to offer support. Stephen's father had been a problem drinker so his mother relates strongly to Helen's predicament.

Six months later, low self-regard and the acceptance of sole responsibility for the poor marital relationship leads to Helen developing an anxiety neurosis. Helen, the enabler, is unable to function and once more the system enters into crisis. This time, though, Stephen's mother is unavailable through her own ill health and so Stephen has to take time off work. A consultation with the general practitioner, leads to the prescription of minor tranquillisers to control Helen's symptoms. The opportunity to link the marital problems and Helen's resultant anxiety state to the problematic use of alcohol by Stephen is missed. If the linkage had been made, it may have encouraged the role of alcohol to be changed. The stable family system became under threat, but Helen internalised the presenting problem, commenced taking a chemical prop, and the family's alcohol functioning was thus successfully preserved.

Two and a half years later, Stephen has a medical for a new job and this creates the third alcohol-related crisis. His alcohol use is identified as excessive, and a subsequent blood test detects liver damage. The resulting loss of this new job shakes Stephen, as does the knowledge that he has damaged himself physically. He consults his own general practitioner for a second opinion and following this advice he ceases drinking alcohol and experiences only minor withdrawals. Helen happily supports his new abstinence goal and brings to his attention once more her perspective on his problem drinking. With time, the family stabilises and begins functioning with relationships almost identical to those that existed during Stephen's drinking, but there are less problems as the alcohol-related stresses have been removed.

Unfortunately, despite Helen's encouragement, Stephen is inflexible to taking on new interests to fill the time previously occupied by drinking activities. He does not take on any additional parenting roles and Helen is afraid to address this issue for fear of an argument that leads to Stephen drinking again. Both Helen and the children find Stephen difficult to live with as he is surly and seemingly resentful in their presence. This situation continues for five months until Stephen announces that he will start drinking again. He states that he can handle his drinking now and will drink in a controlled way. Within a month Stephen is drinking again at a level similar to his previous drinking pattern.

Helen does not accept Stephen's return to drinking. Her recent experience of running the family without the stresses of alcohol problems made her life easier, although the marriage is still far from perfect. A confrontation with Stephen over his drinking leads to a violent scene. His assault on Helen involves the police and

Stephen leaves the house only to get arrested for drink driving. Helen contacts the social worker previously involved with the family and gains support in dealing with the situation.

The result is that Helen refuses to have Stephen back until he stops drinking. His job is also likely to be lost through the impending removal of his driving licence. These events lead to another crisis for Stephen and he stops drinking once more. After two weeks, Helen allows him to return home, subject to his continued abstinence. He agrees to work with the social worker along with Helen and consequently, he is able, with time and support, to develop new skills for dealing with high-risk drinking situations and alternatives to the time he used to spend drinking. Stephen subsequently lost his job but found another lesser paid one that does not involve driving. Three years later, he is still dry except for a brief two-day relapse and the family have moved on to Level 7, dry, stable, non-problem-drinking behaviour.

Case study summary

The drinking-focused lifestyle of the Jones family lasted twelve and a half years, commencing from the start of Stephen and Helen's relationship and ending after five and a half years of related problems. During this time a number of alcohol-related crises occurred, which presented the family with opportunities to change their alcohol-based lifestyle. Some of these crises involved outside agencies, i.e. social work, general practice, and the police, and the influence of these agencies could have been considerable, had they recognised and given priority in their actions to the drinking problem. Unfortunately, each lost opportunity allowed the continued deterioration in the family's lifestyle. On each occasion, something important was sacrificed by a family member, or the family as a whole, in order to save the family's drink-focused way of functioning.

At any of the crises, the family system could have broken up through separation of one or more family members. In this family example there was no break-up, although on occasions it was threatened. Hence the sequence of events was drawn out and the family deterioration lasted five and a half years, commencing with the first alcohol-related crisis of injury to Trevor and ending with the fourth and last, the injury to Helen.

The involvement of the Social Services Department during the first crisis where the family was placed on the 'At Risk' Register was a major opportunity. The recognition of the role of alcohol in relation to the first child's injury was important and seemed to be adequately taken into account. Unfortunately, the action was not followed through. Soon after the family returned to their drinking lifestyle and the Social Services seemed to accept this state of affairs on the basis that Helen and her mother would protect Trevor. The emphasis on moving the family away from a drinking lifestyle was lost. It took two and a half years for another opportunity, Helen's anxiety state, to present and a similar timespan for a third crisis caused by Stephen's realisation that he was experiencing alcohol-related health problems. Six months on, the fourth crisis occurred through marital violence, at which point Helen contacted her previous social worker from the time of the first crisis.

The social worker's role in the family's alcohol problem has been crucial throughout. By not following through the initial action on the alcohol problem at the time of Trevor's injury, the work the family needed to undertake took five and a half years longer to happen, during which time the family's problems got worse. An aware social worker, consistently pressurising for alcohol change, could well have enabled Helen to be stronger earlier and educated the family about the role of alcohol. Similarly, other professionals, such as the general practitioner or the police, could have achieved some progress if they had been able to focus their attention on the drink problem.

Recruiting 'resistant' families

Having an understanding of the way problem-drinking families function is an important part of being able to help. Most social workers already have some knowledge of family functioning and general skills in intervening in family interaction. The ability to enable families to engage in the necessary change process is similarly important. However, often family members may see the drinking problem as belonging purely to the consumer; this view can present problems for the social worker trying to assist the process.

Stanton *et al.* (1981) and Wermuth *et al.* (1986) have considered these difficulties in detail and have suggested a range of engagement principles that social workers may find helpful to their practice. Below are ten principles adapted from their work.

1. The social worker should decide which family members need to be included and not leave this decision entirely to the presenting client. A partner or a relative, preferably from the same household, is likely to be more influential and informative than a recent friend. In addition, a relative with personal experience of the drinking problems, is more likely to want to be involved. Even if they dislike

the problem drinker, they will be anxious to see the family problems resolved. Steinglass (1987) has reviewed the literature on family-therapy outcome studies and concluded that there is strong evidence to support the view that it is more effective to work with family members and the individual drinker together rather than the individual alone.

2. Whenever possible, one or more additional family members should be encouraged to attend an early interview. Their involvement in the process, not only gives another perspective on the family's problem, but also allows an opportunity to encourage their support in the work ahead.

3. Do not assume that the presenting client will bring in other family members on their own. They may find it hard to involve them, fearing problems may be made worse.

4. Permission to contact other family members should be acted on quickly. Whenever possible the social worker should contact the family during the interview where permission is given. The chances for successful family recruitment are increased as a consequence.

5. The closer the social worker's initial contact with the presenting client is to the first family session, the greater the chances are for recruiting the family.

6. The earlier the social worker enters the chain of 'helpers' encountered by the presenting client and their family, the better the chances of family recruitment. The social worker should, where appropriate, ensure he or she is the primary worker or joint co-worker for the family.

7. The social worker should approach the family with a rationale for their future work that is non-perjorative, non-judgemental, and that in no way blames them for the problem.

8. The rationale for family work should be presented in such a way that, in order to oppose it, family members would have to state openly that they want the problem to continue.

9. The social worker should try to adopt the family's needs and expectations as the primary goals for future work.

10. An important recruitment variable is the extent to which the worker shows interest in the family through his or her willingness to expend considerable effort in engaging them.

General family survival tips

The following are suggestions for social workers who are in contact with family members living with another's problem drinking. They are general points which can be easily conveyed over the phone, or in short, face-to-face interviews.

1. Encourage the family member(s) seeking help to find someone close to them in whom they can confide. The social worker can be a useful short-term aid in this respect but not necessarily a readily accessible one. In reality, 'natural resources' in the community are preferable and should be developed for longer term use.

2. Encourage those contacting you to take into account the needs of other dependants in the family i.e. children. Equal consideration should be encouraged for those others suffering and the presenting client may be able to help others who are suffering as well as him/herself.

3. The client should be encoraged to see him/herself as important in his/her own right, and as having his/her own needs. Often the initial contact will take the form of the family member wanting to save the problem drinker rather than necessarily helping him/herself and fellow family members.

4. Urge honest communication between family members. Those suffering from the problem drinking of others often fail to assert their own needs in order to avoid short-term problems, such as arguments. The member seeking advice and support should be encouraged to be assertive but, in doing so, the safety of the family should be taken into account where violence may occur.

5. The responsibility for continued drinking rests with the consumer. Family members should be encouraged to let the problem drinker take responsibility for his or her own drinking behaviour, i.e. by not covering for mistakes and, where possible, not paying any debts. The problem drinker needs to experience directly the consequences of his or her actions in order to learn from them.

6. Help the contacting family member to come to a definite decision about the family problems and support him or her in whatever action he or she decides to take, subject to it not causing harm to others. In response to alcohol problems, encourage him or her only to threaten courses of action that he or she is prepared to follow through.

7. Promote the avoidance of arguments during periods of active intoxication. The best times to resolve difficulties are when the problem drinker is alcohol-free or relatively sober.

Strategies of help

This section considers the different strategies of help that may be given to different family members according to their needs and the stage at which the problem is being addressed. The stages are broken down into pre-action, action, and follow-up. Pre-action refers to the contemplative stage where members of the family may be concerned about the drinking behaviour of one or more others in their family. The action stage refers to situations where work is taking place to resolve the problem, e.g. the family system is unstable and may be entering or is already in a dry state. The follow-up stage refers to where the family has attained a stable state after action has been taken.

Pre-action

With children

Children tend to be most concerned by the following when they live in problem-drinking families (Morehouse 1979):

They worry about the health of the drinking family member, particularly a parent.

The general unpredictability and inconsistent behaviour of family members may lead to the children developing feelings of anger, insecurity, fear, and distress.

The lack of support from the non-drinking family members, particularly from parents, can lead to a child feeling isolated.

Violence and arguments at home may involve the children. They may see them taking place or they may be the recipients, resulting in severe short- and long-term upset.

The lack of positive attention to the children can lead to feelings of being unloved and unwanted.

Sometimes the children may feel that they are in some way responsible for the problem drinking at home.

Inappropriate behaviour by family members towards the children can cause confusion and fear. This includes sexual abuse.

The loss of friends due to the embarrassing family life.

The communication and expression of these concerns can be difficult for the children to achieve. Trust is, consequently, a particularly important issue which has to be addressed by the social worker through time and consistency. Alcohol information may be effective in allowing the child to understand that the situation is not of their making and this should be accompanied by concrete coping suggestions.

Ensuring that the children do not feel responsible for their parents' drinking can be a difficult task. A major problem is that strictly speaking schools are not allowed to let their pupils see social workers without the permission of parents. This can cause difficulties if the headmaster is adamant about this principle, even though the child may be requesting such help themselves. One possible way around this may be the setting up of an independent advisory and support service for the children of problem-drinking families. Such a service should ideally enable children and adolescents to meet others in the same situation and allow them to be advised and supported by adults with specialist knowledge (Ackerman 1983). The service would fill a considerable gap in the range of services for young people aged under 18 years whose parents are experiencing drinking problems.

With partners

Al-Anon, the family offshoot of Alcoholics Anonymous, offers support and advice to family members in most areas of the country. The Al-Anon groups, though, do tend to focus predominantly on the needs of female partners of male problem drinkers using an illness and disease approach. Consequently, they offer a service that attempts to meet the needs of only a portion of suffering family members. Given an appalling absence of services to family members, Al-Anon have, in effect, a near monopoly on alcohol services to such families. There is a strong need for the development of an alternative to Al-Anon that does not promote a disease approach but one of individual determination, where family members, other than those doing the problematic drinking, are encouraged to act positively for themselves to improve their own lives. A small study into this area by an Alcohol Service in the Northeast suggests that the need is clearly there with one-third of those contacting a service for 'affected others' being partners (Yates 1988). Specialist women's services such as Women's Refuges are in a good position to offer support services to women suffering from living with violent problem drinkers. They offer crisis accommodation and sympathetic short- and long-term support.

With parents

Parents living with their problem-drinking adolescent children or adult children have some sources of advice open to them. Local Councils on Alcohol and Alcohol Advisory Services, as outlined in Chapter 1, are obvious points of support, although some parts of the UK still do not have such services.

Agencies specialising in services for the elderly, such as Help the Aged, Age Concern, and statutory home help services, may be in a stronger position to focus on parents aged over 65 needing support in coping with alcohol-related problems. Their services are clearly provided on a much wider scale and, given the present contact with this age group, they must already be dealing with some people experiencing difficulties from the drinking of their adult children.

Developing the knowledge and skills of social workers to act as alcohol advisors in these agencies would be a helpful first step, in encouraging identification of problems and appropriate agency action.

Sadly, some parents are subject to alcohol-related violence from their offspring – an area which is currently receiving little attention. Local authority or private-sector rest homes may be sources of crisis refuge in these instances, as well as Women's Refuges where appropriate.

During action

With children

The children often find it a major task to adjust to the changes of behaviour that ensue when the family moves away from a lifestyle based on problem drinking. Support for the children can be enlisted through the extended family, where available, or through the provision of individual work or family work. Group work with other children who are experiencing, or have already experienced, the adjustment to family life without alcohol problems may be helpful.

With partners

Partners can be isolated by the actions of the problem drinker. This situation may be purposely engineered to contain the partner and family. The more control the problem drinker exercises, the less chance there may be of the partner gaining support from elsewhere to alter the family problem. Consequently, isolated partners may benefit from partner's support groups – a point not missed by Al-Anon. Marital work can also be useful for couples with poor communication to enable the expression of fears and needs, and social workers will already be familiar with various aspects of intervention in work with couples.

With parents

Mowatt *et al.*'s work (1982) with drug-dependent, young people and their families suggest that, in cases where they are all still living together, the substance problem may serve to divert attention away from other family difficulties that the family seem unable to resolve. Typically, these difficulties are between the parents. The drug-using sibling may seek by their problematic behaviour to diffuse the parental attention from their own difficulties. This means that family work which successfully passes through the drug-user's initial crisis tends to move on to a parental crisis that once more tempts the drug user back into problematic behaviour.

The key is to isolate the sibling from trying to resolve the parental problem for them. The parents have to deal with their own problems and in so doing the drug-using sibling may discard his or her dysfunctional role.

The patterns described in families with drug problems similarly apply to work with families experiencing alcohol problems. Social workers should be watchful for the symptomatic role being passed onto another family member. The family may thus try to avoid dealing with its other major issues, such as marital mismatch. In some cases, the adolescent and young adult siblings may in fact have difficulty leaving the family because of their role in maintaining stability by their problematic use. A key act may well be the eventual separation of the parents from the sibling. He or she may be freed from the family nest and the role of parental rescuer.

Mumey (1984) describes a group for the parents of young people with drinking problems. The group is an adjunct to family work and enables the parents to gain additional support from their peers as well as an outside perspective on their family problems. Few facilities in this country focus on the needs of parents of young problem drinkers and the development of such groups would be a useful addition to the existing range of services.

Follow-up

With children

Planning ahead and coping with relapse in the family can be major issues during this phase. Black (1981) suggests some problem-solving strategies for children who are coping with parents relapsing back to problem drinking. For instance, where father has a drink problem and he has arranged to take his child out, it is useful to get an agreement on courses of action in case of drinking. If father is drinking again and causing difficulties, the child can quote their agreement, for instance, that he or she does not wish to go with father now and that a pre-arranged contact, such as mother, can be asked to collect the child. It is helpful for a child or adolescent to talk through and prepare for possible high-risk situations so that they feel clear about courses of action and that there is already agreement and support for their own assertive behaviour in these drinking situations. The social worker can have an important role in mediating between conflicting family members to achieve these agreements. The social worker may also act as the contact when problems arise and intervene to ensure that the needs of the child or adolescent are met where necessary.

Adult children from problem-drinking families are left with a series of 'life legacies' that can take time to resolve. From her experience of group work with adult survivors from problem-drinking families, Woititz (1983) suggests a number of areas where they may experience emotional difficulties. The survivor may guess at what is 'normality', have difficulty completing plans, lie even when it is safe to tell the truth, be self-critical in the extreme, and may have difficulty in enjoying him/herself as a result of being too serious. They may also find intimate relationships troublesome, over-react to change by others and be constantly seeking approval. Additional difficulties can include feeling different to others, being impulsive, extremely loyal, and either irresponsible or super-responsible. Social workers need to be sensitive to these areas when dealing with adult children of problem-drinking families.

Self-help groups can be a constructive means of helping those damaged from living in alcohol-focused families. Some survivors may be a high risk for developing alcohol problems themselves as a consequence of growing up and learning drinking behaviours in such families. Agencies involved in providing helping services may find it productive to organise groups for such clients. Specialist alcohol services might find it helpful to run groups for those clients who have alcohol problems and who lived themselves as children in families where there were drinking difficulties.

With partners

The impact of the initial action taken on alcohol-related problems may diminish with time for some family members, particularly the consumer. So much so that the problem drinker may not wish to keep to his or her original goals. They may feel that they are not as influential now and that their views are no longer important. If changes in the way the family functions are to be long lasting, it is useful for the partners to feel actively involved. Social workers should encourage partners to regularly review the family's changes to date and determine whether they are on target in meeting the original planned goals. Adjustments may need to be made over such things as child care and finances, and these adjustments should be joint decisions. The social worker may act as helpful arbitrator during such reviews.

Social workers should also encourage partners to look at their own life changes and whether they are gaining an improved level of satisfaction. Their own needs are important. On-going groups for partners can provide long-term support so that when life crises occur, either alcohol or non-alcohol-related, there is support available. In addition, the social worker could be used at times of crisis to support the family.

With parents

Support for parents during follow-up can be very important in preventing the offspring from relapsing back to problematic drinking. A strong relationship between a parental couple can indicate that they can cope and that they do not need their children to rescue them through problem drinking. The parents' new way of functioning is usually tested out at some stage by a return to problem drinking. This return, though, is usually short-lived, subject to the parents having made new ways of coping with family life.

Conclusion

This chapter has examined the range of difficulties that can present in problem-drinking families and I have suggested a framework for understanding the way such families function.

I have put forward the view that the role of the social worker can be influential in the pre-action, action and follow-up phases. And that the use of alcohol-related crises in particular, can lead to dramatic alteration in the functioning of families, giving an opportunity to move away from an alcohol-focused lifestyle.

Contrary to the popular stereotype of 'alcoholics never change', drinking problems can be influenced considerably, even after many years of severe problems, subject to the timing of the concentrated input. Social workers are in an excellent position to assist families to change their alcohol-based functioning.

Social work can assist family members to understand the nature of the lifestyles they have derived and suggest ways of escaping from it. The social worker can encourage and support one or more family members at the times at which they wish to see change take place, and during the follow-up stage. In addition, the social work role may include their active statutory intervention to ensure the welfare of others, which in turn may induce a family crisis. The need to help families resolve their drinking problems and the necessity for legal protective action in families are not incompatible.

The timing of concentrated social work action is important, there is no point in resolving, say, a repeated financial difficulty for a problem-drinking family if they do not act on their alcohol problem. It is a different matter, though, if the family are working on their alcohol use. Hence a social worker who expects substantial

change during a period of chaos will be constantly disappointed –
crises are the way in.

© 1990 Graham Fanti

References

Abel, P.M. (1983) *Alcohol Related Problems in Social Work Caseloads*,
Social Services Department, Avon County Council.

Ackerman, R.J. (1983) *Children of Alcoholics: A Guide for Parents,
Educators and Therapists*, New York: Learning Publications/Fireside.

Black, C. (1981) *'It Will Never Happen to Me!' – Children of Alcoholics*,
New York: Ballantine.

Byles, J.A. (1978) 'Violence, alcohol problems and other problems in
disintegrating families', *Journal of Studies on Alcohol* 39(3):551–3.

Creighton, S. (1984) *Trends in Child Abuse: Fourth Report on the Children
Placed on NSPCC Special Unit Registers*, London: NSPCC.

Gayford, J.J. (1975) 'Wife battering: a preliminary survey of 100 cases',
British Medical Journal 1:194–7.

Jenkins, H. (1989) 'Precipitating crises in families: patterns which connect',
Journal of Family Therapy 11(1):99–109.

Mather, B. (1988) *Child Mistreatment and the Misuse of Alcohol*, Social
Services Department, Devon County Council.

Minuchin, S. and Fishman, H.C. (1981) *Family Therapy Techniques*,
Cambridge, USA: Harvard University Press.

Moos, R.M. and Moos, B.S. (1984) 'The process of recovering from
alcoholism: comparing functioning in families of alcoholics and
matched control families', *Journal of Studies on Alcohol* 45(2):111–18.

Morehouse, E.R. (1979) 'Working in the schools of children of alcoholic
parents', *Health and Social Work* 4(4):144–62.

Mowatt, D.F., Heard, D.B., Steiner, F., Stanton, M.D. and Todd, T.C.
(1982) 'Crisis resolution and the addiction cycle', in M.D. Stanton *et al.*
(eds), *The Family Therapy of Drug Abuse and Addiction*, New York:
Guilford Press.

Mumey, J. (1984) *Young Alcoholics: a Book for Parents*, Chicago:
Contemporary Books.

O'Hagan, K. (1986) *Crisis Intervention in Social Services*, London:
Macmillan.

Orford, J., Oppenheimer, E., Egbert, S., Hensman, C. and Guthrie, S.
(1976) 'The cohesiveness of alcoholism. Complicated marriage and its
influence on treatment outcomes', *British Journal of Psychiatry*
128:318–39.

Parad, H.J. and Caplan, G. (eds) (1965) 'A framework for studying
families in crisis', in *Crisis Intervention: Selected Readings*, New York:
Family Service Association.

Seixas, J. (1979) *How to Cope with an Alcoholic Parent*, Edinburgh:
Canongate.

Skynner, A.C.R. (1976) *One Flesh: Separate Persons, Principles of Marital and Family Psychotherapy*, London: Constable.

Stanton, M.D. and Todd, T.C. (1981) 'Engaging resistant families in treatment', *Family Process* 20(3):261–93.

Steiner, C.M. (1971) *Games Alcoholics Play*, New York: Ballantine.

Steiner, C.M. (1974) *Scripts People Live*, New York: Bantam.

Steinglass, P. (1976) 'Experimenting with family treatment approaches to alcoholism, 1950–1975: a review', *Family Process* 15(1):97–123.

Steinglass, P., Davies, D.I. and Berenson, D. (1977) 'Observations of conjointly hospitalised "alcoholic couples" during sobriety and intoxication: implications for theory and therapy', *Family Process* 16(1):1–16.

Steinglass, P. (1979) 'The home observation assessment method (HOAM): real-time naturalistic observation of families in their homes', *Family Process* 18(3):337–53.

Steinglass, P. (1980) 'A life history model of the alcoholic family', *Family Process* 19(3):211–26.

Steinglass, P. (1987) *The Alcoholic Family*, London: Hutchinson.

Vannicelli, M. *et al.* (1983) 'Family problems related to the treatment and outcome of alcoholic patients', *British Journal of Addiction* 78:193–204.

Wegscheider, S. (1981) *Another Chance: Hope and Health for the Alcoholic Family*, Palo Alto: Science and Behaviour Books.

Wermuth, L. and Scheidt, S. (1986) 'Enlisting family support in drug treatment', *Family Process* 25(1):25–33.

Wilson, G.T. (1984) 'Alcohol and sexual function', *British Journal of Sexual Medicine*, Feb/March, 56–8.

Woititz, J.G. (1983) *Adult Children of Alcoholics*, Pompano Beach: Health Communications.

Yates, F.E. (1988) 'The evaluation of a "Co-operative Counselling" Alcohol Service which uses family and affected others to reach and influence problem drinkers', *British Journal of Addiction* 83:1309–19.

Chapter six

Helping in groups

Ken Barrie

Group work has been a popular method of intervention for using with people who have problems, particularly since the Second World War. The increase in the use of such approaches and their popularity sprang, in part, from economic necessity in that helping agencies were aware of an increasing number of people making demands on their services without the increase in staff required to sustain the same level of individual interventions.

Around the same time the discipline of social psychology identified through research endeavours that people's behaviour in a group was likely to be greatly influenced by that setting. Certain behaviours could be increased and skills enhanced, whilst certain other behaviours could decrease and performance could deteriorate. Despite a gap between the applicability of research findings in the practice setting, research findings gave credibility to the new and developing methods of intervention which fall under the title of group work. The general benefits of group work have been written about elsewhere (Douglas 1976). Thus the use of groups is an established method of intervention for helping people who are experiencing problems in various aspects of their life. Some people experience problems related to their drinking and using group approaches can be an effective way of helping them both to reduce their problems and change their drinking behaviour. This chapter outlines some uses of group work in helping people with alcohol problems, the aims of such groups, and selection of group membership. In addition, methods which have been shown to be effective are outlined and a timetable for a group approach based on these methods is presented.

Alcoholics Anonymous

Perhaps surprisingly, the idea of people with similar problems meeting to discuss them together and supporting each other has been established for a considerable time amongst people with alcohol problems. Alcoholics Anonymous originated in the USA in the mid 1930s in the social context of the ending of prohibition of alcohol in that country (Heather and Robertson 1985), but its roots lie more immediately in the religious meetings of the Oxford Group and the Washingtonians in nineteenth-century America. Once established in the USA these self-help groups flourished and now estimates are made of their membership as being in excess of 1 million people worldwide (see also Chapter 1).

Alcoholics Anonymous has been central to the development of a whole range of self-help groups for people experiencing similar difficulties. Apart from its impact on responses to social problems, its influence on our understanding of alcohol problems and the way in which helping services have responded has been profound. Robinson (1979) noted that in a general population survey AA was considered to be the most useful organisation for someone with drinking problems. Indeed, when statutory and non-statutory organisations began to develop their efforts to help problem drinkers in the 1960s, AA's influence was strongly felt in that clients would be advised about their 'illness' and group interventions would often be very similar to an Alcoholics Anonymous meeting. Many of the helpers, particularly in the emerging non-statutory sector, were active or former AA members. Therefore, by implication the AA approach and style of group intervention spread and developed in new areas of service delivery. It is possible that the extent of this influence resulted in many people believing that problem drinkers got help only in groups, thus perhaps reinforcing the belief of some helpers that they did not have the appropriate skills to help this client group effectively on an individual or family level.

Having outlined the impact of Alcoholics Anonymous in relation to responses to problem drinkers, it is important to clarify what AA does and what happens at the group meetings. Although this particular topic is developed more fully in Chapter 1, it is important, however, to reiterate some of AA's major functions at this point.

One of the main aims of the fellowship's meetings is to encourage sharing whereby individuals identify with one another on the basis of having difficulties in common, namely 'alcoholism'. This is achieved by individuals telling their own story of their problem drinking history thus enabling that individual to share his or her experience with the rest of the group and also for the group to identify with the problem. Robinson (1979) found that AA members found talks, stories, and discussions to be the most helpful aspects of AA attendance over and above business and administrative matters. Active involvement in AA is encouraged and through time an individual's experience of AA will change, from initially seeking support for their own sobriety, to helping others. Thus AA becomes a way of life in terms, not only of length of involvement, but also in terms of having an impact on other spheres of the individual's life (AA 1955). Given AA's belief that alcoholism is an illness or disease, the emphasis is not on 'having alcoholism' but on 'being an alcoholic'. Thus AA views alcoholics as being different from the rest of the population. As alcoholism is regarded as a permanent state, help and support of AA is seen as being lifelong.

The AA approach to alcoholism, then, involves a particular style of group approach but, in addition, it involves the promulgation of a belief system about alcohol problems and a way of life which may maintain sobriety for some problem drinkers. Not all people with alcohol problems will use AA, nor will all who attend maintain lifelong contact.

What group work has to offer the problem drinker

Problem drinkers are likely to benefit in much the same way as other people with problems do in group situations. Whilst there is a great debate in the addiction field as to the effectiveness of intervention or treatment (Saunders 1985), with regard to group work it has been suggested that 'this type of therapy appears to be less costly than individual treatment in terms of staff and money. Almost all research has shown that group therapy is at least as effective as, and less expensive than, individual treatment' (Rose 1986:443–4). Apart from equivalent effectiveness in terms of 'outcome' and cost-effectiveness relative to individual methods, there are a number of other benefits to be gained from the group situation.

1. The experience of being in a group is central to human existence. Given that attitudes and behaviour are largely formed in a group setting, they should also be amenable to change in a similar setting.

2. A group setting is likely to offer problem drinkers the opportunity to see that they are not alone in their difficulties. This is particularly important, as those who develop problems in relation to such a widely used drug, are likely to be stigmatised by family and community alike.

3. The group offers its members a unique opportunity to practise and develop new interactive behaviours in a protected setting.

4. The opportunity is offered to enable members to give and receive both positive and negative feedback with regard to attitudes and behaviour. In addition, feedback from peers is likely to be more acceptable than from the group leader.

5. By giving feedback to others, individual group members become helpers in their own right. This is of great importance in increasing an individual's belief in his or her own abilities, and is important in terms of maintaining any wellbeing gained after the group finishes. Such opportunities also take the focus away from the group leader as the only available helper.

6. The opportunity to give feedback or to reinforce the attitudes and behaviour of others in the group is important within the group and may be generalised to the members' functioning in other social settings. It has been suggested that as a person learns to reinforce others, he or she is reciprocally reinforced by others. As a consequence, mutual approval and liking will increase, as well as group cohesion (Rose 1986).

7. As interaction within the group develops, members are involved in the creation of, and adherence to, a range of uniquely created norms. These norms should function to enhance the initial or agreed aims of the group and, in fact, it is the group leader's task to ensure that this happens. Such norms are powerful and the group will influence members who deviate from the rules, to conform to behaviour surrounding requirements for attendance, forcefulness of feedback, not drinking between meetings (if appropriate), not arriving intoxicated, and maintaining abstinence.

8. The group setting may also offer the opportunity for a more complete assessment of the individual's situation, as they can be observed interacting with other people.

9. People are often vague about the exact nature of their difficulties with regard to drinking. The group setting may offer members the opportunity to identify their problems more clearly and in so doing develop their own self-assessment skills, as well as moving towards resolution of their difficulties.

10. The group setting can also be used to teach specific skills such as social skills and problem-solving techniques (D'Zurilla and Goldfried 1971). In this context the group offers individual members a wide range of persons who can be used as role models. It also provides the opportunity for role playing and behavioural rehearsal. In such a setting the members have the opportunity to practise behaviours which have been identified as potential solutions to problems.

11. Group members may also be used as partners in homework tasks which have been agreed to be completed between meetings.

12. The group setting provides the forum for reporting back and monitoring behaviour and measuring the achievement of agreed tasks between meetings, but it additionally offers the opportunity of assessing change on the basis of the individual's performance in the group.

13. Given the development of a range of norms created by the group, the imposition by the group leader of their own values becomes less easy. Group members are more likely than an individual client to challenge or disagree with the worker's values and opinions.

14. The opportunity is provided to anticipate and effectively prevent difficult and stressful situations which may invite a return to problem-drinking levels.

Some, or all, of these beneficial aspects of group work with problem drinkers will be brought into play depending largely on the aims and structure of the group. Behavioural approaches to groups can be looked upon as a continuum from short-term intervention, which involves training, to intensive, long-term therapy (Rose 1977). At the 'training' end of the continuum, groups focus on the teaching, learning, and development of specific skills. As a result of this and the limited number of sessions involved, a specific agenda is used in each of the group meetings, thus allowing only a limited range of flexibility. At the more intensive end of the continuum, a wide range of intervention methods is used and the group is able to focus more on the situation of individuals. With the increase in time and the flexibility in the nature of the group, the influence of group processes and norms become more important and powerful as therapeutic devices.

Selection: which people for which groups

Anyone who presents at an agency with alcohol-related problems should be helped to participate in an assessment of their situation. There are good reasons for doing this, particularly with people with alcohol problems, as assessment in its own right can be an effective method of intervention. More attention has been paid to this topic in Chapters 2 and 3.

Some people with alcohol problems may not be suited to resolving their difficulties in a group setting. A good assessment will indicate whether the person should be involved in any of a number of methods of intervention or, indeed, referred to another agency. Part of an assessment for group work (or other interventions) should be a detailed outline of the person's drinking behaviour and the problems they are experiencing. The reader is referred to Chapter 1, which outlines the nature and extent of alcohol-related problems, with regard to problems of intoxication, regular, heavy use, and dependence. From Thorley's (1980) classification, it is clear that people may experience difficulties with their drinking in one or more or all the modalities. However, it would be inappropriate to have some group members who might primarily experience problems of intoxication combined with others whose difficulties relate to their inability to refrain from drinking heavily, e.g. an adolescent whose offending was related to being drunk would not be an appropriate candidate to be helped in a group consisting primarily of regular, heavy or dependent, middle-aged male drinkers, who regularly experienced withdrawal symptoms, and vice versa. Table 6.1 outlines client groups commonly found to experience alcohol-related problems and possible aims for such groups.

Table 6.1 Alcohol problems, client groups, and group aims

Alcohol problems	*Common client groups*	*Potential group aims*
Intoxication	Young people	Identifying problems Cutting down consumption Reducing problems
	Offenders	Reduction of problems including offending
Regular use	Wide range including: chronic health problems; frequent GP attenders; general medical patients	Cutting down consumption
	Those at risk in specific occupations such as publicans, seafarers	Abstinence re: certain physical conditions
Dependence	Wide range of clients, commonly 25 years and over	Cutting down/abstinence

Preparedness to change

Almost all helping strategies are based on the assumption that a person wishes to change something about their situation in order to minimise the negative consequences of their behaviour. Despite this, it is not uncommon for those who come into contact with problem drinkers to find that some people do not appear to want to change their drinking behaviour. Additionally, some of those who do stop or cut down return to their previous pattern of problem drinking rather sooner than intended. Prochaska and Diclemente (1983) have suggested that people with drug problems, and other problem behaviours, can be categorised on the basis of their thoughts and actions into several different stages in the behaviour change process. Given that problem drinkers are likely to think and act differently, depending on their preparedness to change, consideration of these stages of change will help identify the extent to which individuals might be prepared to change their drinking behaviour. By implication the appropriate strategies which may be employed in a group can be identified, as well as clarifying what sort of group might be useful to a particular individual.

The stages of change are as follows:

1. Pre-contemplation
2. Contemplation
3. Action
4. Maintenance
5. Relapse

For further details of these stages of change and their development, see also Chapter 3.

Pre-contemplation

'Pre-contemplators' are those who use the least change strategies (Prochaska and Diclemente 1983). In effect, they identify the benefits of their drinking or drug taking which outweigh the problems and difficulties. They do not notice or seek out information which may advise them about alcohol-related problems and what may be done about them. Pre-contemplators are likely to feel that they do not have any problems which require changing or may view the problem as being about something or someone else. They may also indicate that they feel that there is little point in being in the helping situation. Such individuals traditionally have been seen as having problems of denial or being unmotivated. However, it is important to take into account their view of the world, if they are to change at all. Offers of help whether in a group or any other setting would, on the face of it, seem to offer little to such individuals. However, they are not uncommon and may well be in contact with a social worker in relation to child care, family, or offending problems. As a consequence they may be suitable group members in that the group setting may offer clients an opportunity to reassess their situation and consider the extent to which alcohol may play a part in their difficulties, whether social, health, or legal.

As pre-contemplators are unlikely to change their drinking

behaviour because of the perceived benefits of such change, there are a number of aims which may be attempted in the group setting.

First, the opportunity is given to offer information on the impact of alcohol on the drinker's health, and of the social and legal consequences related to drinking. Given that drinking behaviour is likely to continue, the second aim is to enable individuals to examine their health and social situation, thus reducing or limiting the damage which might accrue through continued drinking. The third aim is to attempt to alter the client's motivation by identifying possible reasons for drinking and establishing the links between that behaviour and any difficulties or life events which may have been experienced (e.g. court appearances, health problems, the reception into care of a child). It may be more appropriate to deal with pre-contemplators in a group by themselves. However, care should be taken when including them in a group with those at the 'contemplation' and 'action' stages, as pre-contemplators may influence such a group negatively by disagreeing that alcohol is a problem and denying that change may be required.

Contemplation

'Contemplators' are those at the stage in the process of change who are considering the need to do something about their drinking. They will be currently using alcohol perhaps quite heavily, but will be dissatisfied with that situation. They are likely to look for information about alcohol, e.g. posters or pamphlets and are likely to feel that their regular use of alcohol makes them disappointed in themselves. Contemplators are also likely to think that they are ready for change. Despite this there is also a sense of reluctance to change drinking behaviour; they are likely to experience conflict between the positive and negative aspects of their drinking.

Contemplators, then, may not yet be ready to change their behaviour but they are ready to absorb information, raise their consciousness about their drinking, and change their attitudes and beliefs about both themselves and their drinking. The broad aims of a group-work intervention for contemplators would then consist of:

1. Providing information on alcohol and related problems as well as advising on the type and range of help available and what such help consists of.

2. Identifying problems which individuals experience in relation to their drinking and considering the costs and benefits of continued or changed drinking behaviour. The aim being to increase

the individual's perception or belief that there is a need to change their behaviour.

Action

Individuals in the action stage use the greatest number of change strategies. They have made the decision to change or stop and will have made such a decision quite recently. Like those in the contemplation stage they are likely to be disappointed in themselves with regard to their harmful drinking. In a very real sense they are changing their opinions and beliefs about themselves. Individuals at this stage will tell themselves that they can succeed at changing their drinking. They are also likely to find it very useful having social workers and other group members who will support them in their continued behaviour change and in whom they can confide. They are also likely to have arranged to take up alternative activities instead of drinking when they want to relax or wind down.

The aims of a group designed to respond to those in the action stage will include: maintaining and increasing an individual's commitment to his or her changed behaviour. Also developing strategies to help participants change their behaviour e.g. by problem solving and realistic goal setting. Implicit in this approach to persons in the action stage is the need to develop relapse prevention strategies i.e. to maintain changed behaviour. In adddition, however, it is important to prepare for the possibility of relapse and in this sense management of a relapse is an important aim.

Maintenance stage

Those at the maintenance stage will have changed their drinking behaviour for quite some time (Prochaska and Diclemente 1983). Despite this they still use change strategies to maintain their situation. They are still likely to be vigilant of situations which can be difficult, such as meeting old drinking friends or visiting particular public houses and will actively remove things from their physical or social environment which remind them of the problematic behaviour. Like those at the action stage, they will engage in alternative activities to drinking heavily, when they wish to relax or socialise.

The main aims of a group-work response for those at this stage would be first, to maintain commitment to the changed behaviour or way of life and, by implication, to prevent relapse and plan the management of relapse. Focusing much less on drinking behaviour results in overall lifestyle change being a major aim in a group at

161

Table 6.2 Stages of change and appropriate interventions in the group setting

Stage	Strategies of change	Appropriate intervention strategies in groups	
		Group aims	
Pre-contemplation	Benefits of drinking perceived rather than costs. Strategies used less than those in other stages.	1. Reduce harm	(a) Information on health maintenance and consequences re continued drinking
			(b) Identify any problems
		2. Increase commitment to change	
		3. Give information	(c) Emphasise links between drinking and adverse life events e.g. court appearances, child-care issues
Contemplation	Consciousness raising e.g. 'I look for information.'	1. Increase consciousness of problems	(a) Information on health and social consequences
			(b) Record and monitor problem drinking behaviour
	Self-re-evaluation e.g. 'My regular use of alcohol makes me feel disappointed in myself.'	2. Increase commitment towards behaviour change	(c) Identify problems and facilitate expression of concern
			(d) Facilitate change of self-perception and attitudes to harmful drinking
			(e) Advise on the nature of 'help' for problem drinkers
Action	Self-re-evaluation Self-liberation e.g. 'I tell myself I am able to do it if I want to.'	1. Maintain and enhance commitment to change	(a) Facilitate identification of problems
			(b) Facilitate the expression of extent of concern by the client
	Helping relationship e.g. 'I have someone who listens when I want to talk. . . .'	2. Change behaviour	(c) Enhance perception of the need to change
			(d) Set realistic and achievable goals
	Reinforcement management e.g. 'I am rewarded by others if I don't. . . .'		(e) Teach problem-solving methods
	Counterconditioning e.g. 'I do something else instead when I want to relax.'	3. Teach prevention and management of resolution breakdown	(f) Identify benefits of change for participants
	Stimulus control		(g) Identify harm-free behaviours
Maintenance	Stimulus control e.g. 'I remove things that remind me of. . . .'	1. Maintain behaviour change	(a) Maintain commitment to new behaviours
			(b) Encourage development of new lifestyle/activities
	Counterconditioning	2. Prevent/manage relapse	(c) Encourage vigilance over risky situations
		3. Encourage lifestyle change	(d) Encourage environmental change
Relapse/failure of resolution	A combination of contemplation and action	1. As contemplation and action stages	As contemplation and action stages

this stage i.e. taking up new activities, changing relationships, and creating a new way of life. Attendance at Alcoholics Anonymous provides such a function fo some individuals.

Relapse

Individuals at the relapse stage when they have been involved in a bout of drinking or where their resolutions have broken down (Allsop and Saunders 1987), also use change strategies. Despite the conventional wisdom of relapse being seen as a failure or being 'back to square one', the opposite is the case, in that individuals at this stage of change use a range of change strategies which seems to be a combination of those used in the contemplation and action stages (Prochaska and Diclemente 1983). This means that relapse is very much an active part of the process of change and is consequently an appropriate focus for a group-work approach. The main aims of such a group would be a combination of those used in both contemplation and action, the aim being to move individuals from thinking about changing their drinking behaviour to doing something about it. (See Table 6.2).

A group programme for those who wish to change their drinking behaviour

As we have seen, not all people who experience problems from their drinking wish to change their drinking behaviour. Those who do, regardless of the extent or severity of their problems, have usually come to perceive the benefits of drinking as being outweighed by the costs (Saunders and Allsop 1986). Two major problems then face a group which has come together to change their drinking behaviour. The first is to maintain and enhance the belief that the extent of the problems and the concern felt about them, warrants some sort of action. This may be achieved by participants being enabled to outline their own perception of their difficulties and to express their concerns about these problems, rather than simply being told what needs to be done by the group leader. In this sense 'a person is more likely to integrate and accept that which is reached by his or her own reasoning processes' (Miller 1983:160).

The second problem area is that given that the group participants' commitment to change remains high, how do they then cope with the wide range of difficult situations and emotions which will present themselves and would normally have been 'solved' by drinking? In other words, how might relapse or failure of resolution be prevented?

Given the high 'failure of resolution' amongst problem drinkers, and the rest of the population, in day-to-day situations, such as breaking New Year's resolutions, the fact that participants are highly likely to drink at some future date needs to be built into such a programme (Allsop and Saunders 1987). Given the myriad of potentially 'dangerous' situations for an individual, let alone a group, it is not possible to teach individual skills for every single risk situation. What is possible, however, is to teach problem-solving skills which are generaliseable, i.e. once they have been learnt they can be applied to a wide range of problematic situations (D'Zurrilla and Goldfried 1971). Indeed, it has been suggested that problem drinkers are poor problem solvers (Heather and Robertson 1985). Studies indicate that two years after formal treatment, one of the major contrasts between 'survivors' and 'relapsers' was the extent to which problem-solving and coping skills were employed (Billings and Moos 1983).

In essence, then, a group intent on changing drinking behaviour needs to have the opportunity to maintain and enhance their resolution to change, as well as to learn and practise new methods which may reduce the risk of a return to harmful drinking. As a consequence of these needs, the group leader's role will range from the commonly acknowledged group-work skills of facilitation in relation to enhancing commitment and belonging to the group, to those of educator and tutor in relation to teaching problem-solving methods and rehearsal of specific behaviours. The need for members to use the learning from the group is emphasised. It has been noted that 'performance based interventions more readily achieve both behaviour and attitude change than do purely verbal procedures, in other words, the problem drinker should have practice in doing the things necessary for a change in lifestyle' (Rollnick 1985:140).

The following timetable, or group agenda, has been designed to be implemented in five sessions with each session lasting about 2 to 2½ hours. However, the structure is flexible and it may be appropriate to deal with some issues over a longer period of time. As mentioned previously, consideration should also be given to the nature of the client group for which the programme is intended – those with problems of intoxication, regular, heavy use, or dependence.

Aim

To enable participants to change their problematic drinking behaviour.

Objectives

1. To help identify problems related to drinking.
2. To maintain and enhance a commitment to change drinking behaviour.
3. To teach methods of resolving drinking problems.
4. To monitor drinking behaviour.
5. To prevent a return to problem drinking.
6. To help cope with a lapse.

Session one

The main task of this session, apart from making people feel comfortable and welcome, is to focus on people's concerns about their drinking problems. By identifying their problems and expressing their concerns, it is likely that an individual's 'commitment to change' or motivation will be enhanced. By implication, the perception of a need to change drinking behaviour will be clearer. It will be appropriate in some instances to split the group into small discussion groups of two or three to maximise the opportunity to talk about an individual's concerns.

The following topics should be covered:

1. Discussion on an individual's expectations of the group. Clarification of some basic rules, for example, turning up sober.
2. What problems are experienced in relation to drinking? How much? Where? When? With whom? What consequences? Discuss in small groups. Encourage participants to identify the problems they experience in relation to alcohol. An emphasis should be placed on describing problematic drinking and drinking behaviour in its social context and identifying the positive and negative consequences.
3. Allow participants to express their own concern about their problems.
4. Participants should be enabled to consider the costs and benefits of their drinking behaviour. On the basis of such an analysis, individuals who decide that change is necessary will be supported by the group.
Homework Ask the participants to identify a situation which is likely to result in their starting to drink.

Session two

This session is concerned with participants discussing situations which are likely to result in their drinking heavily and also looking at the consequences. Problem-solving skills should be taught in order that participants may develop skills which will enable them to change their behaviour and break the link between difficult situations or feelings and drinking and its harmful consequences.

The following topics should be covered:

1. Feedback from the group regarding the 'homework' from the last session.

Participants should be encouraged to identify situations which precede heavy drinking. As such they may be defined as risky or problematic situations. The link between risky situations or negative emotions and subsequent drinking and problems should be emphasised.

2. Teach problem-solving skills in line with the following:

Rationale Making decisions is a general part of life and a problem-solving difficulty is deemed to exist when an individual has no effective response to a specific situation or related set of situations.

Orientation Problems are viewed as things to be solved – not a confused mess over which the client has no influence. Problem solving is a skill which can be learned.

Definition It is essential that a client's 'problems' are clearly defined. 'My marriage is a mess' is not soluble – but 'My spouse objects to the time I spend at the pub' may have a solution. Precise definition, followed by 'prioritising' is necessary.

Generation of solution What are the possible specific solutions to each specific problem? The use of brainstorming techniques without any criticism, indeed the more wild the ideas the better – they often generate novel solutions. The focus is on quantity breeding quality.

Decision making Which of the possible solutions are attractive to the client? Which does he or she wish to pursue?

Verification Joint assessment of chosen solutions either by 'thinking through' or actual practice to determine whether a solution is likely to be effective (Allsop 1987).

3. Enable the group to rehearse problem-solving skills by using each individual's high-risk situation. Such 'risk' situations could include: very strong emotions such as anger, anxiety, depression, or conflict with partners or being offered drinks by friends.

By following this procedure all participants should leave the group with a range of potential solutions, other than drinking, to a specific problematic situation.

4. Participants should have the opportunity to rehearse the behaviour which has been identified as a potential solution.

Homework To use problem-solving skills and carry out the solutions or goals which were decided upon.

Session three

This session will consist of identifying the extent to which participants have used the problem-solving skills and how useful this was in terms of identifying solutions and achieving goals which were decided upon. Participants should be encouraged to rehearse problem-solving methods again within the group and rehearse behaviours which have been identified as potential solutions or goals. Problem solving may also be used effectively to resolve interactional difficulties within the group, such as dominance and conflict in interaction amongst members, which adversely influence the therapeutic aim of the group.

The following topics should be covered:

1. Feedback from the participants regarding their attempts to use problem-solving skills and achieve goals set.
2. Were goal behaviours achieved fully, in part, or not at all?
If the goals were achieved, then the participant should receive reinforcement from the rest of the group. If the goal was not achieved, then it is important to identify the barriers to success. Rehearsal of specific goal-achieving behaviours should be encouraged.

Homework Carry out specific goal-oriented behaviour.

Session four

Once again participants' efforts and achievements should be reviewed since the last meeting. Given the high likelihood of participants' drinking, perhaps problematically at some future date, the approaches already taught should now focus on managing a return to problematic drinking rather than trying to prevent it. No attempt should be made to reinforce the notion that heavy drinking is acceptable, but that it is likely to occur and will be worth being prepared for, thus preventing a few drinks developing into problematic drinking.

The following topics should be covered:

1. Feedback from participants regarding homework from the previous session.
Use of problem-solving techniques if there is an identified problem in relation to goal achievement.
2. The possibility of drinking in the future should be introduced and participants' views on the consequences sought, if they did use alcohol again. Some resistance can be expected in raising this subject, particularly if participants are committed to abstinence.

3. The focus of the group's concern should be on how harmful effects might be minimised. In this context a problem-solving approach would be appropriate. Participants may wish to take notes to which they can refer in the future.

Homework   To negotiate with friends or relatives what sort of help and support they may be able to offer should drinking become problematic again.

Session five

The main function of this session is to review the participants' progress and identify what they require next. Such a review should involve recapping on their perceived need for change in their drinking behaviour, thereby maintaining and enhancing the need to change behaviour or to maintain and build on achievements already made.

The following topics should be covered:

1. Feedback from homework agreed in the previous session.

2. Recap on reasons for wishing to change behaviour. Participants should be enabled to reflect on the reasons selected for wishing to change in the group's first session and the extent to which they have achieved their aims.

3. On the basis of this discussion, the future of the group, if any, or its membership can be agreed. Some may feel the need to continue meeting whilst others may consider that they require something different in order to maintain and develop their situation.

Conclusion

To conclude, then, the use of groups for problem drinkers as well as other people experiencing difficulties is well established. Group work may offer a cost-effective method of responding to some problem drinkers who are in contact with helping agencies, often in considerable numbers. The nature of problems and characteristics of the individual will to some extent define the aims and objectives of a group response. Similarly, an individual's preparedness to change will enable him or her to become a member of an appropriate group with aims coinciding with his or her needs. A wide range of tested and effective intervention methods may be used in the group setting, thus enhancing the already powerful impact of group norms and processes on an individual's behaviour.

© 1990 Ken Barrie

References

Alcoholics Anonymous (1955) *Alcoholics Anonymous*, 2nd edn, New York: World Services Inc.

Allsop, S. (1987) *Relapse Prevention and Management Therapists' Manual*, Paisley College, Paisley: Alcohol Studies Centre.

Allsop, S. and Saunders, W. (1987) 'Relapse: a psychological perspective', *British Journal of Addiction* 82(4):417–29.

Billings, A. and Moos, R. (1983) 'Psychosocial process of recovery among alcoholics and their families: implications for clinicians and programme evaluations', *Addictive Behaviours* 8:205–18.

Douglas, T. (1976) *Groupwork Practice*, London: Tavistock Publications.

D'Zurilla, T. and Goldfried, M. (1971) 'Problem solving and behaviour modification', *Journal of Abnormal Psychology* 78:107–26.

Heather, N. and Robertson, I. (1985) *Problem Drinking: The New Approach*, London: Penguin.

Miller, W.R. (1983) 'Motivational interviewing with problem drinkers', *Behavioural Psychotherapy* 11:147–72.

Prochaska, J. and Diclemente, C. (1983) 'Stages and processes of self change of smoking: towards an integrative model of change', *Journal of Consulting and Clinical Psychology* 51:390–5.

Robinson, D. (1979) *Talking Out of Alcoholism: The Self Help Processes of Alcoholics Anonymous*, London: Croom Helm.

Rollnick, S. (1985) 'The value of cognitive behavioural approaches to the treatment of problem drinkers', in N. Heather, I. Robertson and P. Davies (eds) *The Misuse of Alcohol: Crucial Issues in Dependence Treatment and Prevention*, London: Croom Helm.

Rose, S.D. (1977) *Group Therapy: Behavioural Approach*, Englewood Cliffs, NJ: Prentice Hall.

Rose, S.D. (1986) 'Group methods', in F. Kanfer and A. Goldstein (eds) *Helping People Change: A Handbook of Methods*, 3rd edn, New York: Pergamon Press.

Saunders, W. (1985) 'Treatment doesn't work: some criteria of failure', in N. Heather, I. Robertson, and P. Davies (eds) *The Misuse of Alcohol: Crucial Issues in Dependence Treatment and Prevention*, London: Croom Helm.

Saunders, W. and Allsop, S. (1986) 'Giving up addiction', in F. Watts (ed.) *New Developments in Clinical Psychology*, Chichester: Wiley.

Thorley, A. (1980) 'Medical responses to problem drinking', *Medicine* (3rd series) 35:1816–22.

Name index

Subject index